REVISE EDEXCEL GCSE (9–1)
Drama

REVISION WORKBOOK

Series Consultant: Harry Smith

Author: William Reed

Notes from the publisher

While the publishers have made every attempt to ensure that advice on the qualification and its assessment is accurate, the official specification and associated assessment guidance materials are the only authoritative source of information and should always be referred to for definitive guidance.

Pearson examiners have not contributed to any sections in this resource relevant to examination papers for which they have responsibility.

For the full range of Pearson revision titles across KS2, KS3, GCSE, Functional Skills, AS/A Level and BTEC visit:
www.pearsonschools.co.uk/revise

Contents

A small bit of small print
Pearson publishes Sample Assessment Material and the Specification on its website. This is the official content and this book should be used in conjunction with it. The questions in this book have been written to help you practise the knowledge and skills you will require for your assessment. Remember: the real assessment may not look like this.

Key roles in the theatre

> **Guided**

1 Look at Figures 1–3, which show the key theatre roles. Identify each role. Then annotate each photograph, summarising the key skills and responsibilities for each.

In the exam, you will need to consider how theatre is made from three different perspectives: the roles of **performer**, **director** and **designer**. Think about the skills involved in each role, and what each role is mainly responsible for.

(a)   Role:

....

Interpreting and developing character

Figure 1 In this role, a range of skills is used to convey narrative and plot to an audience.

(b)   Role:

....

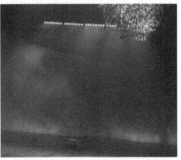

Figure 2 People in this role tend to specialise in different aspects of the production.

(c)   Role:

....

Figure 3 This role includes overall creative control of a production.

2 Read through the different elements listed in the table below. For each, indicate whether the performer, director or designer has primary responsibility for that element by completing the 'Key role' column.

	Element	Key role			Element	Key role
a	Develop characterisation.			**d**	Lead the production team to create an overall vision for the production.	
b	Produce a range of initial ideas for the lighting, costume, sound or set.			**e**	Use facial expression to convey emotions.	
c	Give detailed feedback to the performers during and after a rehearsal.			**f**	Consider which colours would best convey different atmospheres to an audience.	

The audience

> **Guided**

1 Complete the paragraph below to describe the role of the audience. Use words from the box to fill in the gaps.

~~production team~~	director	themes	performer
designer	centre	perspective	audience

The audience should be placed at the .... of every decision made relating to a

performance. It is the responsibility of the entire production team to ensure the play successfully

communicates key .... and the agreed purpose to an audience. Decisions such as

where a performer is positioned on stage, or the way a line is delivered, can have a powerful

impact on an ...., controlling their reaction. Each role within the production will

consider different things. A .... may ask how they want the audience to feel about the

character they are portraying. A .... may ask how they want the audience to react to

the choices made relating to lighting, costume, sound or set. A .... will consider where

the audience may be positioned and what impact this will have on their .... of the

events on stage.

2 Look at the three factors below. For each factor, write a brief paragraph to explain why this can affect decisions about the target audience.

(a) Content and material: ....

....

....

(b) Language: ....

....

....

(c) Themes and issues: ....

....

....

3 Read the play outline below. Explain who the target audience might be for this play. Give reasons for your answer.

> It is important to be clear about who a production is aimed at. Think carefully about who your target audience would be in light of these factors: content and material, language, and themes and issues.

> An old man loses his wife and returns to an empty home. His two children are both grown up and lead very busy lives. They live a long way from their father and rarely see him. The man becomes extremely lonely, sometimes spending days without speaking to anyone. The audience are encouraged to think about what they can practically do to support someone who is lonely. The play is linked by a series of monologues, spoken by the old man at different times of his life. The language changes to reflect his age and also the era in which he is living.

....

....

....

....

Theatrical concepts

> **Guided**

1 Look at the anagrams below. Unscramble the words to reveal different theatre concepts.

   (a) GREEN *genre*

   (b) COPS REMIX ....

   (c) DECREASING TO SIT ....

   (d) OF MR ....

   (e) EL STY ....

   (f) CURE STRUT ....

   (g) TIN GAGS ....

   (h) NEXT COT ....

2 Read through the list of theatrical concepts in the table below. In your own words:

   (a) Define each concept.

   (b) Describe how it can affect a production.

> In the exam, you need to show your understanding of theatrical concepts. Make sure you are familiar with a wide range of concepts and the impact they can have on a production.

Concept	(a) Definition	(b) Impact on performance
Social, historical and cultural contexts		
Stage directions		
Genre		
Staging		

3

Conventions and terminology

1   The table below lists **four** conventions that are often used in making theatre. For each convention, give an example of how it can be used practically, and describe the impact it may have on an audience.

> Theatre conventions are techniques for communicating ideas to an audience. In the exam, you need to use the most appropriate technical vocabulary when discussing your ideas.

Convention	Practical use and impact on an audience
Directly addressing the audience	
Symbolism in costume and set	
Use of multimedia (such as music and projection)	
Use of multi-role (where a performer plays more than one character)	

Guided

2   The concept map below gives four reasons why it is a good idea to use the correct vocabulary and terminology when discussing different aspects of theatre-making.

For each reason, explain why this is important when answering questions in the exam.

To ensure my answers are strong

....
....
....
....
....
....
....

To prove my knowledge and understanding of theatre-making

Using the correct terminology indicates that I have grasped different ideas and concepts. Also, that I have a clear understanding about the things I am talking about, whether these are ideas relating to the actual performance or the themes of the play.

Why using technical terminology is important

To communicate my ideas and intentions clearly, and to avoid confusion

....
....
....
....
....
....
....

To show my understanding of the different roles in theatre-making

....
....
....
....
....
....
....

The performer

Guided 1 Complete the sentences below to describe the role of the performer. Use words from the box to fill in the gaps.

designers	audience	physical	interpretation
text	~~communicate~~	directors	ensemble

A performer uses a range of skills to *communicate* with an audience, including vocal skills,

.... skills, characterisation and use of space. During rehearsals, performers will often

work with .... and .... to create a successful performance. A performer will

also usually work as part of an ...., being an effective member of a team. They will

need to develop their own .... of a character, as well as exploring the ....

in as much depth as possible. However, the most important thing for a performer to consider is

the relationship they develop with the ....

2 Complete the following table to show which tasks are the primary responsibility of the performer and which are the primary responsibility of the director. Use a tick (✓) to show your answers.

> When staging a production, tasks will be shared out. The responsibility may not always rest with just one person. Here, think about who is **primarily** responsible for the task.

Task	Primary responsibility of	
	the performer (✓)	the director (✓)
Communicating character		
Engaging with the audience		
Creating an overall vision for the performance		
Applying the overall vision in performance		

3 Read the extract below.

ELIZABETH: This is your mess. I want nothing more to do with it. [*Exits*]

[KAREN *is left, staring at the box fearfully. She looks around to ensure she is alone and moves to check there is no one at the door. She moves back to the box and picks it up. She then takes the box and exits.*]

Explain **one** way you would perform the role of Karen. You will need to consider the context of the scene and the characters' intentions, as well as the stage directions that are given.

....

....

....

....

....

....

....

....

Tone and intonation

> **Guided**

1 Voice is an important performance tool. Name **four** things that voice can convey to an audience.

(a) Emotions

(b) ....

(c) ....

(d) ....

> Being clear about the difference between tone and intonation is very important in the exam. Try to use a range of adjectives to describe both tone and intonation, such as 'clipped', 'accusatory' and 'light-hearted', which will make your ideas clear.

2 In your own words, describe the meaning of the following terms.

(a) Tone: ....

....

....

(b) Intonation: ....

....

....

3 Read the extract below.

> ROBERT: Finally! You've made it. We have been so worried about you. Where on earth have you been? We have been worried sick. Why didn't you phone to tell us where you were?

When performing the extract, how would you use tone and intonation to show these **two** different emotions?

(a) Concern/worry: ....

....

....

(b) Anger: ....

....

....

4 Read the extract below.

> GEETA: Just put the bag down over there, underneath the window. You must be careful with it – don't bash it or let it drop. Tell me – is it heavy?

When performing the extract, how would you use tone and intonation to show these two different emotions?

(a) Hopelessness: ....

....

....

(b) Enthusiasm: ....

....

....

Pause and pitch

Guided 1 What sort of information can voice help to communicate about a character? List them below.

(a) Their age – for example, very young, young, very old.

(b) ....

(c) ....

(d) ....

2 Read the extract below.

> ERIN: I'm not sure what to say…
> ROSE: You're supposed to help me. You can't be lost for words.
> ERIN: Wait.

(a) If you were playing the role of Erin and decided that she was very nervous and scared, where could you place a pause in the first line to reflect this? Mark the place in the extract above with a forward slash ('/').

(b) Justify your decision.

....

....

....

....

3 Decide on a context for the extract above. Then explain how you would use pitch and pause to help convey your intended meaning to an audience.

> Consider who is saying what, and why. Think about the emotional state of the characters, as well as the relationships between them. This will put the scene into **context** and help you decide what it is you wish to communicate to the audience.

....

....

....

....

....

....

....

....

....

....

....

....

Clarity and pace

1 Read the extract below. Set in 1802, a young woman from London is convicted of theft and sentenced to transportation to Australia.

> [MARY JOHNSON, *aged 19, stands in the dock of a courtroom, distraught and sobbing while the* JUDGE *delivers the verdict and sentence for her crime.*]
>
> JUDGE: Mary Johnson. You have been found guilty of the theft of two overcoats from the household of Thomas Baker, where you worked as a servant girl. You will be taken from this courtroom and held at the county gaol until such a time as you can be transported to Sydney Cove, Australia, for a period of seven years.
>
> MARY: No! Please, Sir. Please don't send me to Australia. I'm needed here to look after my brothers. Please, Sir. Let me stay here. I didn't do it. Please! Please! Please!
>
> [MARY *is taken away from the dock by two Police Officers.*]

(a) Explain how you would use vocal clarity to deliver the lines of the judge.

> Vocal clarity is changed by many different vocal techniques, such as pitch, pause and volume. Use these to help make your point.

....

....

....

....

....

....

....

(b) How could you use pace to deliver the repeated words 'Please! Please! Please!' at the end of Mary's line?

....

....

....

....

....

....

....

(c) Explain how you would use vocal clarity and pace in Mary's lines to contrast with those of the judge.

....

....

....

....

....

....

....

Accent and inflection

Guided

1 What sort of information can a specific accent help to communicate about a character or play?

(a) Character status

(b) ....

(c) ....

(d) ....

2 Look back at the extract on page 8, and then read the information below.

> At the end of the play, the cast take on the roles of different political prisoners who were transported to
> Australia and other penal colonies. They tell the audience about their experiences and the conditions they
> faced. These political prisoners were made up of the following groups of people:
> - Scots rebels
> - Yorkshire rebels
> - British naval mutineers
> - Canadian rebels
> - The rebels from the Merthyr Tydfil (Wales) Rising
> - Irish rebels

Explain how you could use accent to help the audience understand the identity of each of the
different groups mentioned above.

> Sometimes the location of a play is vital to the overall presentation or interpretation of the performance.
> At other times, location is not important and does not add to the narrative in any way. As a performer,
> consider whether your interpretation of character would benefit from using an accent.

....

....

....

....

....

....

....

....

....

....

3 Read the extract below.

> You actually thought this was a good idea

Notice there is no punctuation. Explain how you would use inflection to make this line into a:

(a) Question: ....

....

....

(b) Statement: ....

....

....

Emphasis and volume

1   Read the extract below.

> ANDREW: I think there is a solution.
> MARIE: I just don't know how this could have happened. How could she do this and then just leave?
> ANDREW: We can't worry about that now. Let's just work out what we need to do and then get started.
> MARIE: You don't understand. I trusted her.

In each case below, explain what impact putting a stronger emphasis on the words in **bold** would have on the meaning of the line.

> Remember that **stress** and **emphasis** mean the same thing.

(a)   ANDREW: **I** think there is a solution.

This means that Andrew himself believes that there is a solution to the problem.

(b)   ANDREW: I **think** there is a solution.

....

....

....

(c)   ANDREW: I think there is a **solution**.

....

....

....

2   How could different volume levels impact on Marie's last line?

> Sudden changes in volume can have a significant impact on the interpretation of a character.

(a)   If the line were shouted, it could show that: ....

....

....

(b)   If the line were whispered, it could show that: ....

....

....

3   The following words can be used to describe volume or tone.

Complete the table below by writing either 'Volume' or 'Tone' next to each word.

> Remember: **tone** describes how lines are said to convey meaning; **volume** refers to how loud or quiet the voice is.

Quiet	Volume	Whispering	
Booming		Softly	Volume
Diminuendo		Nasally	
Monotone		Crescendo	

Diction and nuance

 1 Read the extract below.

> ALI: You must know where you put it.
>
> KELLY: I can't remember. It was here – I'm sure it was.
>
> BREANNA: Where did you go after you left the room? Did you take it with you?
>
> KELLY: No. I put it down here, on the table, and then, after hearing the door slam, I went into the back room. But I didn't take it with me.

Describe how you could use nuance to show the following situations.

(a) Context 1: Kelly is terrified of Ali and Breanna:

If I were playing Kelly, I would speak the first line with a slight stutter on the word 'I'm' to show fear. I would then speak the second line with pace and energy to show I was trying to get all of my explanation out before being interrupted. I would then give a slight pause before saying, quite definitely, 'But I didn't take it with me'.

(b) Context 2: Breanna and Kelly are working together:

....

....

....

....

....

....

2 Look at the anagrams below. Unscramble the words to reveal different words used to describe diction or nuance.

> Using the correct technical language can help you make your point clearly.

(a) CURTAIN OIL AT ....

(b) UNICORN PAIN TO ....

(c) ELF COIN TIN ....

(d) THIN ....

(e) HAD GINS ....

(f) CARET ....

(g) CAUTION NINE ....

(h) INTO US EGGS ....

3 The following words can be used to describe diction or nuance. Complete the table below by writing either 'Diction' or 'Nuance' next to each word.

> **Shading** is a subtle hint of an emotion in the voice.

Shading	Nuance	Inflection	
Enunciation		Articulation	Diction
Pronunciation		Trace	
Suggestion		Hint	

Facial expression and body language

⟩ **Guided** ⟩ 1 Complete the concept map below to show the different emotions that can be conveyed through facial expression.

Fear

....

....

Emotions conveyed through facial expression

....

....

....

....

2 Read the stage directions below.

> [*A loud 'crash' as a door is kicked in.* SHAHEERA *turns abruptly to face the direction of the door and is relieved to see that it is her friend,* CARLOS.]

If you were playing Shaheera, what body language would you use to convey her changing emotions? Give a reason for each point you make.

> Consider how the context affects the character's reactions. Remember to look for as many clues as possible within the given text.

....

....

....

....

....

....

....

....

....

....

3 Choose a significant moment from your performance text. Take one of the characters from the moment and explain how you would use facial expressions and body language to convey the key messages to an audience.

....

....

....

....

....

....

....

....

....

Gesture and proxemics

> **Guided**

1 Describe how you could use proxemics to show the following.

(a) High status: Place the highest status character upstage, looking downstage and separate to the other characters on stage.

(b) Love: ....

....

(c) Hate: ....

....

(d) Fear: ....

....

2 As a performer, describe the gestures and proxemics you would use for the following situations.

> Being clear about the context of the scene will help you decide exactly what the character is trying to communicate. Remember that gesture is only one element that can be used to convey information. Body language, facial expression and vocal skills are also vital in communicating ideas.

(a) | A character is furious with a group who have forced their way into his house. He demands that they leave. The context is serious.

....

....

....

(b) | A character has been tortured and is begging for mercy. The context is serious.

....

....

....

(c) | A character is chasing a man she is madly in love with. However, he manages to get away from her. The context is comedy.

....

....

....

(d) | A group of people gleefully plan a trap for a high-status character who has made their lives very difficult. The context is comedy.

....

....

....

Stance and stillness

> **Guided**

1 Identify **six** types of information that stance can convey about a character.

(a) Status

(b) ....

(c) ....

(d) ....

(e) ....

(f) ....

2 Which of the following is another term for stance? Tick (✓) the correct answer.

(a) Stillness ☐   (b) Position ☐

(c) Posture ☐   (d) Physique ☐

3 Describe **two** scenarios in which a character might be still. Provide a reason for each of your answers.

> The choices a performer makes to portray a character are often affected by the performer's interpretation of that character. For your performance text, you need to use your knowledge of the play and of the context to help you develop your own interpretations about the characters. You also need to be clear about why you have come to those interpretations.

(a) Scenario 1: ....

....

....

....

(b) Scenario 2: ....

....

....

....

4 Choose **two** moments from your performance text when a character or characters could use stillness to convey an important point to the audience. Explain each of your choices.

(a) Moment 1: ....

....

....

....

(b) Moment 2: ....

....

....

....

Movement and spatial awareness

Guided 1 Which of the following words can be used to describe movement? Tick (✓) to show your answer.

> In the exam, you will be asked about how you might interpret a particular character from your performance text. Indicating how you would like a character to move on stage will provide clarity and meaning to your answer.

Stagger		Creep		Trot	
Volume		Scramble		Edge	
Tumble		Burst	✓	Plod	
March		Crescendo		Stammer	
Amble		Dash		Glide	

2 Read through the phrases in the boxes below. Draw lines to match up the phrases so they make sense.

> You can match up the phrases in different ways. However, make sure there is a logic to your answers and that the type of movement is consistent with the situation the character is in.

	How…	**Where…**	**Why…**
	tumbled	from upstage left	joyfully and full of love.
	skated	across centre stage	fearfully hiding from the burglar.
He/She…	crept	downstage	determined to give the child a serious telling off.
	strode briskly	to upstage right	from a combination of being pushed and falling down the slope.

3 As a performer, how could you use spatial awareness to communicate to an audience that your character is frightened?

> Spatial awareness can be a useful technique to communicate different **emotions** to an audience.

....

....

....

....

....

....

....

....

....

....

....

Personality and purpose

⟩ **Guided** ⟩ 1   Read the following list of words that could be used to describe a character's personality. Some of the words relate to a positive personality trait while others indicate a negative personality trait. Indicate which trait is which by writing 'P' for positive or 'N' for negative next to the word.

> Being able to describe a character's personality can help you to express your thoughts and ideas about them. Aim to have a clear understanding of the personalities of the characters in your performance text.

> Look up the meaning of any word you aren't sure about.

Interfering		Sincere		Vengeful		Understanding	
Obstinate	N	Truculent		Versatile		Aloof	
Philosophical		Witty		Pompous		Modest	
Indiscrete		Compassionate		Amiable	P	Self-centred	

2   Choose **three** characters from your performance text and complete the following table. For each character:
  • list **three** key characteristics
  • describe the character's purpose within the play.

Character	(a)	(b)	(c)
Personality trait 1			
Personality trait 2			
Personality trait 3			
Purpose in play			

3   Take **one** of the characters from your answer to Question 2. Using the plot of your performance text, give examples that indicate how each of the personality traits you have listed helps to support the character's purpose or objective at a specific moment in the play.

....

....

....

....

....

....

....

....

....

Motives, aims and objectives

> **Guided**

1 In your own words, write a definition of the following words/phrases.

(a) Aims and objectives: What the character wants or needs to achieve in either a scene or over the whole play.

(b) Motive: ....

....

2 Read the scenarios below. For each one, consider what motive the character might have for their actions. Write down your ideas.

> You also need to consider why the characters in your own performance text behave the way they do. Think about whether their motives stem from something that happens elsewhere in the play or at the precise moment the specific action takes place.

(a) | A man keeps sending gifts to a woman. |

....

....

(b) | A local politician gathers his corrupt officials together to tell them to smarten up the town ahead of a visit from a high-ranking official. |

....

....

(c) | A homeless orphan steals some fruit from a market stall. |

....

....

3 Select **two** characters from your performance text. For each character, list **three** aims and objectives they have in the play. For each aim/objective, give an example to justify your opinion.

Character name:
(a)
(b)
(c)

Character name:
(a)
(b)
(c)

Development and relationships

Guided 1 Add in the missing words below so that the completed sentence provides a definition of the term **character development**.

evolves	play	~~development~~	beginning

Character development refers to the way in which a character .... and changes from

the .... to the end of the ....

2 Take **three** different characters from your performance text. Add to the table below to show how each character develops over the course of the play. Write a brief description of the character at the beginning, the middle and the end of the play.

> If a character does not appear throughout the whole play, consider how they develop from the start of their own appearance in the play.

Character	Beginning	Middle	End

3 Select **one** of the characters you described in Question 2.

(a) Identify a key relationship that affects your chosen character's development.

....

(b) Write down **three** words to describe that key relationship.

> Using a range of words to describe a relationship will help make your ideas and opinions much clearer in the exam.

....

(c) Explain the role of this key relationship in your character's development.

....

....

....

....

....

Research and impact

Guided

1 (a) Create a concept map to show the different aspects a performer could research to help develop their performance.

> Remember: there is a range of aspects relating to a play that will help a performer produce a more focused, solid performance. For example, researching a character's backstory (what happened to them before the beginning of the play) can help the performer understand the role better.

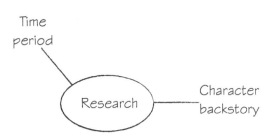

(b) Expand the concept map you created for Question 1 (a) to include details and examples relating to your own performance text. Add as many points as you can to each category.

> For example, for *The Crucible*, the time period would be 1692, and the character types might include high-status religious leaders, rich landowners and vulnerable villagers.

2 Choose **two** characters from your performance text. Explain the impact you would like them to have on the audience when they first appear.

> Think carefully about your character in light of the concept map you created above. How are they affected by this context?

(a) Character name: ....

Impact when first enters stage: ....

....

....

(b) Character name: ....

Impact when first enters stage: ....

....

....

Still images and asides

1 Identify the **two** features that a performer would **not** use to create a still image. Tick (✓) the correct answers.

Body language	☐	Gesture	☐	Stillness	☐
Audience awareness	☐	Voice	☐	Silence	☐
Mime	☐	Levels	☐	Proxemics	☐

> **Guided**

2 Describe **three** different ways in which a performer could indicate to an audience that they are delivering an aside.

> A performer should always consider how they fit into the performance as a whole. Understanding the way they are communicating with an audience (such as using an aside) can ensure the required message is clearly conveyed. For example, think about where the performer is in relation to the audience, where they are on stage in relation to other characters and any gestures they might make.

(a) By facing the audience and directly addressing them when speaking

(b) ....

....

(c) ....

....

3 Choose a key moment from your performance text and imagine you are performing a chosen character from that moment. Explain how you could use **still image** to convey the character's emotions to an audience. Consider how the character is feeling at that moment in the play.

> While you will focus your answer on one character in detail, remember to refer to the other characters on stage.

....

....

....

....

....

....

....

....

....

....

....

....

....

....

....

Monologue and physical theatre

1 Give **three** examples of approaches that can help make an effective monologue.

(a) ....

....

(b) ....

....

(c) ....

....

2 In your own words, write a definition of **physical theatre**.

> Make sure you have a clear understanding of different theatrical styles and their key features.
> For example, a key feature of physical theatre is large amounts of **movement**.

....

....

....

....

....

....

Guided

3 Explain how you could use physical theatre to represent the following situations and events.

(a) **An arrest:** An arresting officer moves towards the person being arrested. The performers engage in a sequence where the officer tries to grab the accused, who then maintains contact with the officer's body but slides around the officer's arms and legs to represent resisting arrest.

(b) A disagreement: ....

....

....

....

....

(c) Love: ....

....

....

....

....

(d) Vandalism: ....

....

....

....

....

Narration and multi-role

Guided   1   List **eight** things a performer can change to indicate they are using multi-role.

(a) *Voice*

(b) ....

(c) ....

(d) ....

(e) ....

(f) ....

(g) ....

(h) ....

2   Read the extract below.

> KOFI: Suddenly, there was silence. For a while, Katie wasn't sure if that was because everything was actually silent – or if the explosion had taken away her hearing. Slowly, she opened her eyes and dared to look up. She was surrounded by dust and smoke. Papers fluttered down from where the house had stood and filled the sky above her. Ash fell like snow around her. She tried to move. First she tried her arms, which she used to push herself up. Then she carefully tried her legs. She felt a sharp, stabbing pain in her left ankle and, as she cried out in pain, she knew that her hearing was slowly coming back. In the distance, she realised she could hear the sounds of sirens. As she pulled herself upright, she began to check her pockets for her mobile phone. It was gone. She tried to call out, but the smoke was too thick, making her choke and gag whenever she took in a breath. She knew she needed help and she knew there was little time. With desperation, Katie began to drag herself towards the sounds of the sirens. And as she did, she heard a familiar voice calling out her name…

Explain how you would play the role of Kofi to emphasise his role as the narrator.

> Always consider how the narrator fits into the structure of the play. For example, is the narrator completely separate from the other characters or is he/she part of the action throughout the play? Consider how the narrator might interact with other performers on stage – as well as the different aspects of performance that might help the performer, such as voice, visibility/position, movement and physicality.

....

....

....

....

....

....

....

....

....

....

....

....

....

....

Mime, flashback and flash forward

> **Guided**

1   Are the following statements about mime true or false? Put either a tick (✓) or a cross (✗) in the columns next to each statement to show your answer.

	Statement	True (✓)	False (✗)
a	Mime uses no words at all.	✓	
b	Mime can be used by only one person at a time on stage.		
c	Mime should clearly represent actions or events through physical movement.		
d	Mime often combines controlled use of facial expression, body language, gesture and movement.		

2   Explain why a mimed sequence might be used in a performance.

....

....

....

....

3   Give an example of when you could use flashback or flash forward in your performance text.

> Think of a key moment in your performance text that could be enhanced by the use of flashback or flash forward. In particular, consider the beginning and end of the play, as well as the transitions between scenes/acts.

....

....

....

....

....

....

....

....

....

....

....

....

....

....

....

....

....

....

Symbolism and split scene

Guided > 1 Explain how a performer could use **symbolism** to convey the following emotions and themes.

> Think about how a performer could use elements such as movement and gesture.

(a) Love: A performer could symbolise love through gesture, such as raising a hand to their chest and laying it over their heart.

(b) Hate: ....

....

(c) Disgust: ....

....

(d) Wealth: ....

....

2 Read the following extract. The split scene has all characters on stage at the same time.

> [A bus stop. AMAR and JIMMI are talking. JIMMI is wearing a new, biker-style leather jacket.]
>
> AMAR: You're looking sharp. Is that a new jacket?
>
> JIMMI: Yeah. I bought it to impress Jenni. It cost a fortune but I heard she is really into the biker look.
>
> AMAR: So this is it? You're really going to ask her out? Finally! After all this time?
>
> JIMMI: Absolutely. She's all I've ever dreamed about. When she sees me in this jacket, she is going to fall at my feet!
>
> [A café. DAWN is drinking a milkshake and JENNI has a black tea.]
>
> DAWN: So you can't have milk because you are a vegan? When did you decide that?
>
> JENNI: Look. I've been doing a lot of thinking. We, as humans, are so cruel to animals. I just need to do something. And if you are going to go veggie, you may as well do it properly.
>
> DAWN: ...but vegan? What about those nice boots you wanted?
>
> JENNI: Yes. Absolutely. No meat, no milk and no leather shoes or jackets. And if anyone can't accept it then I don't want them in my life anymore!

(a) Explain how you would play Amar to aid the impact of the split scene for an audience.

> Make sure you don't take focus away from the main action.

....

....

....

....

....

(b) You are playng Jenni. Explain how you would play the character to aid the impact of the split scene for an audience.

....

....

....

....

....

Caricature and choral speaking

Guided

1   Name **five** techniques that could help to make choral speaking effective in performance.

> Remember that **choral speaking** is when more than one person speaks or reads text at the same time. It can be used to emphasise or underline key moments on stage.

(a)   Clarity

(b)   ....

(c)   ....

(d)   ....

(e)   ....

2   Read the definition of **caricature** below. Then fill in the missing words using the words from the box.

Caricature is an .... of a character's features. As a performer, therefore, you need to

consider which aspects of a .... you want to exaggerate, to give the .... a

clearer understanding of the character's .... in the play. For example, you may have

a character with a lot of .... energy or who is afraid, and you could highlight this

through exaggerated use of .... or over-the-top reactions.

audience	nervous	exaggeration	function	movement	character

3   Identify **two** characters from your performance text that could be portrayed as caricatures. Explain how you would play each character, indicating which performance skills you would use.

(a)   Character 1: ....

....

....

....

....

....

....

....

(b)   Character 2: ....

....

....

....

....

....

....

....

The director

1   Complete the sentences below to describe the role of the director. Use words from the box.

designers	vision	team	style
genre	communicate	performers	creative control

A director has overall *creative control* of the performance. During rehearsals, directors

will often have to work with .... and .... in order to create a successful

performance. The director also needs to lead the .... and be an effective team member

at the same time. A director will develop a creative .... for the play and be clear

about the .... and .... they want to use in the production. One of the most

important things for a director to consider is the key points of the play they wish to convey and

how they can .... these to an audience.

2   Complete the following table to show which tasks are the primary responsibility of the designer, and which are the primary responsibility of the director. Use a tick (✓) to show your answers.

> When staging a production, tasks will be shared out. The responsibility may not always rest with just one person. Here, think about who is **primarily** responsible.

Task	Primary responsibility of	
	the designer (✓)	the director (✓)
Creating an overall vision for the performance		
Producing final costume designs		
Organising and running rehearsals		
Providing the performers with detailed feedback to aid improvements		

3   Read the extract below.

> ELIZABETH: This is your mess. I want nothing more to do with it. [*Exits*]
>
> [KAREN *is left, staring at the box fearfully. She looks around to ensure she is alone and moves to check there is no one at the door. She moves back to the box and picks it up. She then takes the box and exits.*]

Choose **one** of the following production elements:
*   lighting   *   sound   *   props/stage furniture.

As a director, discuss how you would use the production element you have chosen to bring the extract to life for an audience.

....

....

....

....

....

....

....

Messages and subtext

1   As a director, list **four** key messages you would want to convey to an audience about your performance text. For each message, given an example from the performance text.

(a) ....

....

(b) ....

....

(c) ....

....

(d) ....

....

2   In your own words, define the meaning of **subtext**. Include an example.

> As a director, you need to identify each character's objectives clearly. This will help you to locate examples of subtext, allowing you to consider all possible ways (including performance and design) to convey the subtext to an audience.

....

....

....

....

....

....

Guided

3   Read the extract below.

> [DAVID *enters the room and hands* SALLY *a bag.*]
> SALLY: I am glad you made it on time.

Now read situations a–d in the table below. Each situation has a different context. Write down what you think the subtext of Sally's line ('I am glad you made it on time') might be for each situation.

	Situation	Subtext of the line 'I am glad you made it on time'
a	The bag has been stolen. Sally is trying to return the bag before the owner realises.	'I'm glad we can put this bag back before I get into trouble.'
b	The bag is a birthday present for Sally's boss.	
c	The bag contains life-saving medicine for Sally's father.	
d	The bag contains a presentation that Sally needs for an interview. However, David is late and Sally has missed her opportunity to get the job.	

Genre and style

> **Guided**

1 The terms below are related either to genre or to style. Complete the table by writing 'Genre' or 'Style' next to each word.

Epic theatre	Style	Black comedy	
Political satire		Physical theatre	
Romantic comedy		Naturalism	
Social thriller		Historical drama	
Expressionism		Mystery	

2 (a) Identify the genre of your performance text.

Performance text: ....

Genre: ....

(b) Complete the following table by:
  - describing **three** features of the genre you have identified
  - giving examples from your performance text to support your answer.

> Be clear about which features belong to which genre. Understanding this will help you to make appropriate decisions as a director about key aspects of the performance, such as performance and design style, key messages and staging.

Feature of the genre	Example from performance text

Types of staging

> **Guided**

1 Draw lines to link the different types of staging to the descriptions of where the audience is positioned.

Traverse stage	The audience are only on one side of the performance space.
Theatre-in-the-round	The audience are on two sides of the performance space.
Promenade theatre	The audience are on three sides of the performance space.
Proscenium arch	The audience surround the performance space.
Thrust stage	The audience move around the performance space.

2 Imagine you are going to direct a scene that involves the following scenery:

- A tree
- A park bench
- A litter bin

For each type of staging in the table below, draw a stage plan and indicate where you would place each item of scenery on the stage. Give a reason for your answer.

> Always consider your audience when thinking about how to use each type of staging.

	(a) Thrust stage	**(b) Traverse stage**
Stage plan (drawing)		
Reasons for chosen plan		

Consistency and communication

1 Imagine you are directing a production of your performance text. As director, you have decided to stage your play in a traditional style.

> Staging a play in **traditional style** means your performance will reflect the time period in which the play was originally written or set.

   (a) Complete the following sentences.

   (i) The name of the play I am directing is ....

   (ii) The time period/era in which the play was originally set is ....

   (iii) The type of staging I will use is ....

   (b) Indicate **three** ways in which you would ensure unity of convention in your production.

> Remember: **unity of convention** is about making the different aspects of your production consistent. Thinking carefully about consistency will help you produce a more detailed response in the exam.

   (i) ....

   ....

   ....

   (ii) ....

   ....

   ....

   (iii) ....

   ....

   ....

Guided 2 As director, how would you convey the following scenarios to an audience? Explain each answer.

> Remember that directors must work with both performers and designers to communicate ideas and create the impact required. As a director, you need to outline your ideas and intentions for aspects such as movement, lighting, sound, set and costume to the specialists who will make them happen.

   (a) | The scene is taking place at night. |

   Working with the lighting designer, I would flood the stage with a pale blue light, giving the impression of moonlight.

   (b) | Two characters are on stage; Character 1 thinks Character 2 is being very stupid. |

   ....

   ....

   ....

   (c) | There is a considerable difference in wealth between two contemporary characters. |

   ....

   ....

   ....

Purpose

> **Guided**

1　Link each type of purpose to the correct definition.

a	The purpose of the play is to **question**.

b	The purpose of the play is to **challenge**.

c	The purpose of the play is to **educate**.

d	The purpose of the play is to **entertain**.

e	The purpose of the play is to **empower**.

f	The purpose of the play is to **influence**.

g	The purpose of the play is to **encourage understanding**.

i	The play encourages the audience to dispute and question situations and people in power.

ii	The play provides the audience with an escape from the stresses of everyday life.

iii	The play presents the audience with the consequences of different actions, encouraging them to query things around them.

iv	The play encourages the audience to look at different perspectives and tries to shape their opinion.

v	The play encourages the audience to think about the characters and issues, and to develop empathy and understanding of the situation.

vi	The play shows the audience how people can make a real difference and demonstrates how they might go about changing things.

vii	The play engages the audience at a deep level and teaches them about issues and situations.

2　(a)　Write down the name of your performance text and then describe its purpose in no more than 15 words.

Name of performance text: ....

The purpose of my performance text: ....

....

(b)　In the space below, create a concept map to provide the evidence that justifies your answer to Question 2(a). Write 'Evidence of purpose' in the centre of your map.

> Having a clear understanding of what the playwright intended and the original context of the play will provide you with a lot of information about the intended purpose of your performance text.

Managing the audience

> **Guided**

1 Fill in the missing words below to describe the different ways a director manages audience reaction. Use the words in the box to fill the gaps.

action	context	critical	disappointment
genres	~~perspective~~	purpose	reaction
released	resolution	tension	~~view~~

Perspective: A director may choose to give the audience a greater view of the action than some characters in the play. This can give the audience a wider perspective on what is going on and help them to put the action into a better ....

Purpose: A director being clear about the .... of the play is vital. This is not just linked to comedy, but to all styles and .... Clarity of purpose is important to performers, designers and the director, and can be a helpful tool in managing the audience ....

Climax: This is when the .... builds up significant amounts of .... When that tension reaches a .... point, it is then released, often suddenly and with explosive consequences.

Anticlimax: Similar to climax, the tension builds and is .... However, with anticlimax, the .... is less explosive than expected, often leaving the audience feeling unfulfilled or with a sense of ....

2 Read the extract below.

[VICTORIA, *aged 87, walks across the stage. A* YOUNG MAN, *intent on mugging her, is chasing her. As she tries to escape, she falls…*]

How could you direct this scene to make the audience shocked, or to make them laugh?

Consider the full range of performance and design techniques, including vocal and physical skills, sound, lighting, set and costume. Which would help you to manage the audience most effectively?

(a) Shocked: ....

....

....

....

....

....

(b) Laugh: ....

....

....

....

....

....

Choosing location and time

> **Guided** 1 List **four** reasons why a director may change the original location of a play.

(a) To make the play relevant for a modern audience

(b) ....

(c) ....

(d) ....

> **Guided** 2 List **four** reasons why a director may change the original time period in which a play is set.

(a) To make a point regarding a historic issue

(b) ....

(c) ....

(d) ....

3 Think about your performance text. Give **two** advantages and **one** disadvantage for a director of choosing to set the play first in the past and then in the future.

> Think carefully about the impact a change in time period might have on a modern audience. For example, setting a play in the past might create a useful distance from the action, while setting it in the future could make it more relevant for a younger audience. Make sure you include clear references to your performance text in your answers.

Performance text: ....

(a) Setting the play in the past:

Advantage 1: ....

....

....

Advantage 2: ....

....

....

Disadvantage: ....

....

(b) Setting the play in the future:

Advantage 1: ....

....

....

Advantage 2: ....

....

....

Disadvantage: ....

....

Contexts

Guided 1 List and define the **three** different contexts that can affect how a play is interpreted.

(a) Social context – this reflects what is happening to ordinary people at the time the play is set.

(b) ....

....

(c) ....

....

2 Read the summaries of Play A and Play B below. For each play:

(a) Identify the social, historical and cultural contexts.

(b) Briefly describe how each context would influence your interpretation of the play as a director.

> Think about what messages you want to communicate to the audience.

PLAY A	Summary: Set in industrialised East London in 1942. It describes the experiences of four young women working in a munitions factory.	
	(a) Contexts	**(b) Influence on my interpretation as director**
i Social		
ii Historical		
iii Cultural		

PLAY B	Summary: Set in Sharpeville, South Africa, 1960, during the apartheid regime. During a peaceful protest against the racist Pass laws, the police open fire on protestors and 69 people are killed. The play focuses on the impact on one family who lose a loved one.	
	(a) Contexts	**(b) Influence on my interpretation as director**
i Social		
ii Historical		
iii Cultural		

Mood and atmosphere

Guided 1 Read the paragraph below. Use the words from the word box to fill in the gaps.

production	elements	message
feels	~~mood~~	emotions
communicated	context	audience

Mood is the term used to describe how a scene or moment within a .... makes the

audience feel. It has strong links to the .... being .... to the audience.

Mood is often created by different theatrical .... working together. Some of these

elements include vision, ..., location and the .... of the performance.

Atmosphere is similar to mood, but it is more closely linked to the emotions of the

.... Therefore, the atmosphere can be considered to beewhat the audience

.... as a result of the mood of the scene.

2 As a director:

(a) Describe how costume can be used to create a humorous atmosphere.

(b) Describe how set can be used to create a mysterious atmosphere.

> Consider how different elements of design work together to create a specific mood or atmosphere.
> For example, low-level lighting, using a mixture of dark greens and blues, when combined with an
> ominous soundtrack, can create a frightening and tense atmosphere. This can help to make the audience
> fearful of what is about to happen on stage.

(a) Costume and humour: ....

....

....

....

....

....

....

....

(b) Set and mystery: ....

....

....

....

....

....

....

....

Style

Guided 1 Complete the table below to highlight how naturalistic and abstract styles have an impact on **three** aspects of a performance: set, costume and lighting.

> Remember: a **naturalistic style** is a look and feel that resembles real life; an **Abstract style** attempts to express ideas and feelings through elements such as colour and shape.

		(a) Naturalistic style	(b) Abstract style
i	Set	Feature 1: Set looks like the real location of the scene. Feature 2: Set is highly detailed. Example: A scene set in a wood may use an assortment of trees; the floor may be covered in fallen leaves.	Feature 1: Set represents the location using symbolism. Feature 2: Set may represent more than one place. Example: Wooden planks can represent trees in a wood. The planks can be rearranged and moved to represent something different, such as a building.
ii	Costume	Feature 1: Feature 2: Example:	Feature 1: Feature 2: Example:
iii	Lighting	Feature 1: Feature 2: Example:	Feature 1: Feature 2: Example:

2 Label Figures 1 and 2 below to show whether they use a naturalistic or abstract style.

> Always take as many different performance and design aspects into consideration when deciding whether a particular production is naturalistic or abstract in style.

Figure 1 ....   Figure 2 ....

Presenting location and time

1 Describe **two** different ways you could represent each of the locations below.

> Remember to consider how different styles, such as naturalistic and abstract, may affect your ideas.
> Also, make sure you think about how the location should look and sound.

	(a) Hospital	(b) Mechanic's garage
i		
ii		

Guided

2 As a director, how could you present an office, a street and a prison cell in these different time periods: 1540, present day and 2150? Complete the table to show your ideas.

> Think carefully about the time period you need to represent, and make sure you present it consistently.

	Location	Time period		
		(a) 1540	(b) Present	(c) 2150
i	Office	Old-fashioned desk and chair. Quill and parchment. Candle.	Desktop computer and screen. Open plan. Plastic swivel chairs.	Bright lighting. Futuristic moulded plastic chair. Transparent touch screen instead of desktop computer.
ii	Street			
iii	Prison cell			

Staging and blocking

Guided 1 Look at Figure 1, an incomplete stage plan. Identify the areas of the stage using the labels.

~~DSL – downstage left~~	US – upstage	USL – upstage left
CS – centre stage	USR – upstage right	SL – stage left
DSR – downstage right	SR – stage right	DS – downstage

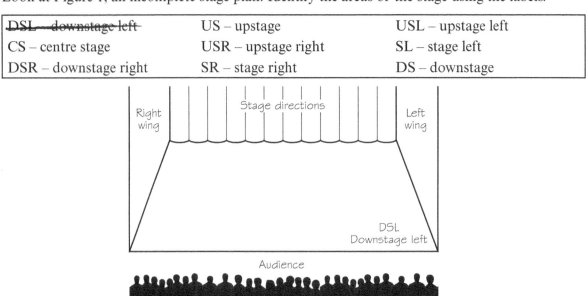

Figure 1

2 Look at stage plans A–C below. Each contains a blocking problem. Examine the positions of the performers and set, and then identify what the problem is. Offer a solution to each one.

> When you are planning the blocking of a scene, always consider audience awareness. For example, be careful not to place performers behind large parts of the set where members of the audience cannot see them.

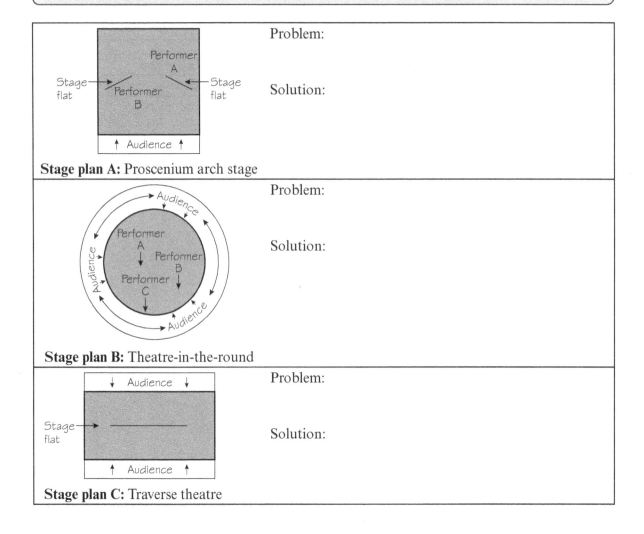

Stage plan A: Proscenium arch stage

Problem:

Solution:

Stage plan B: Theatre-in-the-round

Problem:

Solution:

Stage plan C: Traverse theatre

Problem:

Solution:

Stage business, relationships and proxemics

1   Read the situations outlined below. For each character, describe a piece of stage business the performer could use to enhance the action for an audience.

> Think about the finer details of a character. Also, remember to consider what props and stage furniture might be on stage and which may help the performer.

(a) | A man is feeling intense pressure under difficult questioning. |

....

....

....

(b) | The owner of a clothes shop is angry about the way she has been spoken to by a customer. |

....

....

....

(c) | A young woman, playing a trick on a friend, is trying to stop herself from laughing out loud. |

....

....

....

> Guided

2   Read performance notes (a) and (b) below. Then, in the role of director, annotate the stage plans to show where you would position the performers. Use a letter (A, B) to indicate each performer and an arrow to indicate which way they are facing.

> Think carefully about the relationships between the characters on stage. Remember, proxemics can also be affected by the type of staging used in the performance, as this directly affects the perspective of the audience. Always take this into account when considering where to position the performers.

Performance notes:

(a) | A and B have just had a huge argument. |

(b) | A has just proposed marriage to B, but B is in love with someone else! |

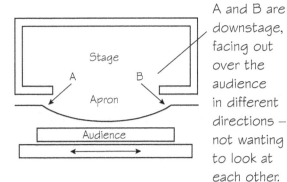

Figure 1 Proscenium arch stage

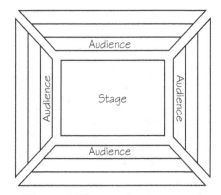

Figure 2 Theatre-in-the-round

Characterisation and style

> **Guided**

1 As a director, what questions would you ask to help formulate your ideas about a character? Complete the concept map below with your ideas.

....

....

Who are they? What sort of person are they?

(**Character information**)

....

....

....

....

> **Guided**

2 Read the information about plays A–C below.

In the role of director, note down how you would want a performer to deliver each character's line of dialogue within the context of the play's central message.

> When thinking about how lines should be delivered, it is important to keep in mind both the central message of the play and the style of the performance.

Play A

Central message	The freedom of the individual versus the power of the state
Style	Physical theatre
Character background	Male, mid 40s. Once had high status but now his power is diminishing.
Character line	'What makes you think you're more important than the rest of us?'
Ideas for delivery	Delivered with sarcasm and anger. Emphasis on 'you' and 'important'. Looks directly at the other characters with hatred and anger, as he is being physically dragged below a group of people who represent a society with higher status than him.

Play B

Central message	Secretly falling in love with someone
Style	Naturalism
Character background	Female, early 20s. Works as a servant for a powerful aristocrat.
Character line	'If you are as lonely as you say you are, perhaps you should consider looking for a companion to talk to.'
Ideas for delivery	

Play C

Central message	Moral responsibility towards those less fortunate
Style	Epic theatre
Character background	Male, mid 40s. High moral status.
Character line	'You could have made a difference to those people, but you chose not to. You chose to take advantage for your own benefit.'
Ideas for delivery	

The costume designer

> **Guided**

1 Complete the sentences below to describe the role of the costume designer. Use words from the box to fill in the gaps.

style	historical	~~consistent~~	research
performers	director	audience	social

A costume designer designs the costumes for a production. They work with the ....

to create costumes that are *consistent* with the chosen .... and characterisation. The

costume designer will carry out .... to ensure the designs are accurate from a range of

different perspectives, such as ...., cultural or .... They will also consider

how costume can help to convey key themes and messages to an .... The costume

designer will produce initial ideas, then develop them into a final design. Finally, the costume

designer will work with the .... to ensure the fit and style are appropriate.

2 Complete the table below to show which tasks are the primary responsibility of the director, and which are the primary responsibility of the costume designer. Use a tick (✓) to show your answers.

> When staging a production, tasks will be shared out so sometimes the responsibility may not always rest with just one person. Here, think about who is **primarily** responsible for the completion of the task.

Task	Primary responsibility of	
	the director (✓)	the costume designer (✓)
Creating an overall vision for the performance		
Producing final costume designs		
Representing the themes and issues of the play through costume		
Working with the performers to ensure the costumes are practical and safe to use on stage		

3 Read the extract below.

> ELIZABETH: This is your mess. I want nothing more to do with it. [*Exits*]
>
> [KAREN *is left, staring at the box fearfully. She looks around to ensure she is alone and moves to check there is no one at the door. She moves back to the box and picks it up. She then takes the box and exits.*]

The director has given you the following information about the extract: 'The performance is set in 1862 and will be naturalistic. Elizabeth and Karen are both young servant girls in a large townhouse belonging to a wealthy family.'

As a costume designer, discuss how you would use costume to engage an audience.

....

....

....

....

....

....

....

Costume and context

⟩ **Guided** ⟩

1 Explain how a costume designer could use symbolism to convey the following emotions/themes.

(a) Love: The costume could be predominantly red, a colour linked with love and passion. Small red hearts could be included in the pattern of a costume for a character who is in love with another.

(b) Hate: ....

....

....

(c) Wealth: ....

....

....

(d) A cold winter: ....

....

....

2 What costumes would these characters wear? Describe them. You could draw or sketch an appropriate costume, with annotations, if you prefer.

> Always try to consider how a costume can reflect information such as the social, historical and cultural context, as well as status and important character traits.

(a) A female military war hero is collecting a medal. The time period is present day.	(b) A prisoner is led from his cell to be executed. The time period is the late 17th century.

Aspects of costume

Guided 1   One element of costume is clothes. What else does costume include? List **four** elements, and then
give **two** examples of each element.

> Think about other aspects of a performer's appearance when they are in character. In the exam, you will
> also need to consider how the different elements of costume work together to create the desired effect.

Element of costume	Examples
Accessories	Handbag, mobile phone

2   Look at the outline of an unfinished concept map below, which shows six different aspects of
costume. Expand on each one by adding as many examples as you can for each aspect.

> There are many different aspects linked to costume. Try to consider things such as colour and weight, as
> well as specific items such as a bag or blusher.

Materials and colours

1 The materials below could be used in a modern costume design. Write down **one** advantage and **one** disadvantage of each material.

> Remember to consider the visual impact and the practical application of each material.

Material	Advantage	Disadvantage
Wood		
Lace		
Metal		
Plastic/PVC		
Cotton		
Leather		
Velvet		

> **Guided**

2 Read the character descriptions below. Decide on the main colours you would use in each character's costume to help communicate the character traits, status and emotions to an audience. Explain your choices in each case.

Character A:

> Puritan minister (1692), very serious and deeply religious. Quite self-centred with high self-importance. Arrogant.

The main costume will be black to signify the role of the character (a religious minister). Black also indicates high status. A white neck collar would signify purity and represent the religious position of the character.

Character B:

> Female teenager (2008). Fashionable and sociable with an outgoing and bubbly personality, but naïve. She has become involved in a problematic situation that is now becoming quite serious and could lead to a lot of trouble for her.

....

....

....

....

Character C:

> Young woman (1912), in her early 20s. Comes from a wealthy family and has been protected from many of the harsh realities of the world. Quite spoilt and self-centred, she is unaware of the consequences of her actions on others.

....

....

....

....

Accessories and masks

1   Look at the character notes below. What accessories would help to communicate information about each character to an audience? Describe your chosen accessories. You can include a sketch with labels/annotations if you prefer.

> Remember to think carefully about the information you are given about the character and the time period. Don't forget to consider the practicality of each accessory.

Character A: Rich and powerful duke, 16th century. Wants to show he has the highest status. Spends a lot of time walking in the city streets.	**Character B:** Rich businessman, 1912. Considers his time is valuable. Enjoys showing his wealth and is always well dressed. Attending formal dinner.
Character C: 15-year-old girl, present day. Spends a lot of her time with a group of friends and is still at school. Is quite fashionable. Likes to be seen with the latest things.	**Character D:** Well-respected professor, 1896. Delivering a lecture to university students. Considers himself of high status and follows the formal traditions of the time.

Guided

2   Complete the concept map below by indicating the different ways in which masks can be used on stage. Give a brief example to justify each of your answers.

To give a character anonymity – for example, masks can be worn to hide their identity from other characters or the audience.

How masks are used on stage

Make-up and hair

Guided 1 Complete the table below.

	Make-up style	Naturalistic or abstract?	Reasons for decision
a	Figure 1 An example of animal make-up	Abstract	The make-up depicts a non-human character.
b	Figure 2 A 2013 production of *Trash Cuisine* by Belaruse Free Theatre		
c	Figure 3 Elizabeth in Act 3 from the 2014 Old Vic production of *The Crucible*		
d	Figure 4 A performer in a traditional Kathakali production (Kathakali is an ancient style of dance drama from India)		

2 Make notes about how you could use hairstyles to present characters a–d to an audience.

(a) Female. 50 years old. High status. She is a rich, fashionable woman who wants to make an impression in society. Looks and appearance are very important to her. Time: 1912.

....

....

(b) Male. 64 years old. Originally high status but lives under a great deal of stress in a city under military occupation. Making an effort over his appearance is a way of defying the regime. Time: 1942.

....

....

(c) Female. 14 years old. Low status. She is quite fashionable, but under a great deal of stress; this is starting to show in a lack of care over her appearance and becoming more scruffy. Time: 2008.

....

....

(d) Male. 20 years old. High status and wealthy background. He has been taught that appearance is very important. He uses his appearance to show his status and fashion sense. Time: 1896.

....

....

Practicality and safety

Guided

1   Describe **three** practical points a costume designer must consider.

> Think: what will help a performer to perform their role effectively, efficiently and comfortably?

(a) Weight – the costume should not be too heavy for the performer to use.

(b) ....

(c) ....

Guided

2   Read these director's notes about a character in the opening scene of a play.

Name: *Joseph Daniels – army messenger* Age: *18* Gender: *Male* Time period: *16th century*	Notes: *Private Daniels has returned from the battlefield to deliver news to the king that his army has been subject to a surprise attack. He has ridden a horse through a terrible thunderstorm, which is still raging. In addition, he was caught in the middle of the attack and wounded in his left arm. However, he managed to fight his way clear.*

As a costume designer, how would you construct a practical costume for this character? Give **three** key ideas in the table below, and note your reasons for each.

> Remember to think about the materials you would use to create a practical costume.

	Practical costume idea	Reasons
a	Aluminium chainmail	Reflects the time period; aluminium is lighter than traditional metals and will make less noise when the performer moves.
b		
c		

3   Read the situations involving costume below. For each, suggest the possible health and safety issues, and how, as a costume designer, you could resolve them.

> Think carefully about how a performer needs to move on stage while in costume. What are the potential hazards for the cast, crew and audience?

	Situation	Potential hazards	Possible solutions
a	A performer in a long, white dress walks through the audience and up five steps to reach the stage.		
b	A large group of performers wearing loose, flowing, lightweight clothing performs an energetic dance on stage. The performance area includes lit candles.		

The lighting designer

Guided 1 Complete the sentences below to describe the role of the lighting designer. Use words from the box to fill in the gaps.

rigging	stage lighting	~~director~~	information
convey	audience	style	programming

A lighting designer designs the .... for a production. The lighting designer

works with the *director* to create a detailed lighting design that reflects the themes and issues

selected by the director. Once the general .... has been agreed, the lighting designer

will consider how lighting can help to .... important .... and highlight key

moments to an .... From this point, the lighting designer will produce initial ideas,

which will then be developed and refined until a final design is produced. The lighting designer

may also supervise the .... and .... of the lights as the design is finalised.

2 Complete the following table to show which tasks are the primary responsibilities of the director, and which are the primary responsibilities of the lighting designer. Use a tick (✓) to show your answers.

> When staging a production, tasks will be shared out so sometimes the responsibility may not always rest with just one person. Here, think about who is **primarily** responsible for the completion of the task.

Task	Primary responsibility of	
	the director (✓)	the lighting designer (✓)
Producing final lighting designs		
Representing the themes and issues of the play through the lighting		
Creating an overall vision for the performance		
Working with members of the production crew to rig and programme the lighting desk to ensure the lighting reflects the intended design		

3 Read the extract below.

> ELIZABETH: This is your mess. I want nothing more to do with it. [*Exits*]
>
> [KAREN *is left, staring at the box fearfully. She looks around to ensure she is alone and moves to check there is no one at the door. She moves back to the box and picks it up. She then takes the box and exits.*]

The director has given you the following information: 'The performance is set in 1862 and is naturalistic. Elizabeth and Karen are both young servant girls in a large townhouse belonging to a wealthy family. It is late at night and there is a clear sky with a full moon outside.'

As a lighting designer, discuss how you would use lighting to engage your audience.

....

....

....

....

....

....

Colour, symbolism, mood and atmosphere

Guided 1 Read the scene descriptions below. For each scene, explain what colours you would mainly use in the lighting design to help emphasise the mood and atmosphere.

> Think carefully about the audience. What is the mood and atmosphere you need to convey?

(a) | A happy ending to a play where many of the main characters pair up and are married.

The stage would be washed with bright, warm lighting, such as yellows and oranges. These would be symbolic of the joy and happiness of the couples getting together and provide the audience with a warm and safe feeling suggestive of a happy ending. This lighting would be enhanced with bright white light to indicate purity and joy.

(b) | An old man is kept prisoner in a military-occupied city. He speaks to a soldier who is keeping guard over him. The soldier ignores the conversation before firing his gun at the prisoner.

....

....

....

....

(c) | Two lovers involved in a forbidden affair are living in a police state. They are arrested by the Secret Police. The arrest is sudden, violent and disorientating.

....

....

....

....

2 Describe how you could use lighting symbolically in the scenarios below to communicate themes/ideas, locations, emotions and moods to an audience.

> Think about elements such as colour and brightness levels.

(a) | A scary ghost story. As the play progresses, individual characters are illuminated. While the characters do not know who will become the next victim, the audience are given a clue just before the death of the next character.

....

....

....

....

(b) | A dense woodland location at noon on a warm, relaxing day.

....

....

....

....

Style, location and era

⟩ Guided ⟩ 1 Look at Figures 1 and 2 below. Identify which style is abstract and which is naturalistic. Then label each image with the key features of the relevant style.

(a) Lighting style: ....

(b) Lighting style: ....

Lighting is generally of equal brightness on the performers, indicating they are in the same room.

Figure 1

Figure 2

2 Describe how you would use lighting to indicate the different locations below.

(a) | An outdoor market in Warsaw, 1942, on a dark, wet early morning. |

....
....
....

(b) | An indoor market in Warsaw, 1942. |

....
....
....

3 Describe how you would use lighting to indicate different time periods below.

(a) | A dining room in a wealthy house in 1832 (evening). |

....
....
....

(b) | A dining room in a wealthy house in 2017 (evening). |

....
....
....

Types of lantern

> **Guided**

1 Match the different types of stage lighting to their descriptions.

a	Soft-edged spotlight		**i**	Gives a lot of light to a wide area on the stage. Very helpful when providing general lighting to large stage areas.
b	Profile spotlight		**ii**	Generally easy to blend into other types of lighting used in the design. Can be used to light or highlight specific areas in the performance area.
c	Floodlight		**iii**	Narrower focus than a flood but a very versatile lamp. Can be used for lighting large areas in colour.
d	Parcan		**iv**	Sharp and clearly defined edge. Excellent when lighting precise spots in a performance area.

2 Look at the situations below. As a lighting designer, explain how you might use different types of lighting to help focus the attention of the audience on specific areas of the stage.

> Think carefully about the audience. Where does their focus need to be at each point? How can you use different lanterns to direct their attention?

(a)

> A group of friends want to play a trick on a bully. They leave a stolen mobile phone on the floor and then hide, waiting for the bully to come along, in the hope that he will pick up the phone and take it.

....

....

....

....

....

....

....

(b)

> An old man is visited by the spirit of a dead friend in the middle of the night. He is terrified by the visit. The spirit is trying to get the old man to change his ways and to make a choice about how his future life will develop. He is presented with three different doors – behind each one is a different future path. The spirit explains what lies behind each door.

....

....

....

....

....

....

....

....

Lighting angles

1   Look at Figures 1 and 2 below. What is the angle of each light? Write your answers in the space below each image.

Figure 1

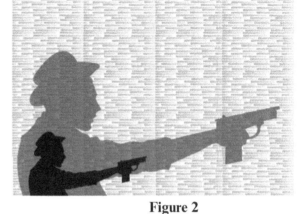

Figure 2

Angle: ....

Angle: ....

 2   Listed below are four different lighting angles. For each angle, describe its main features and uses.

> Always try to consider the impact the angle of the lighting will have from the perspective of the audience.

	Type of light	Main features	Uses
a	High front light	It provides a clear and natural light (similar to the sun or light bulbs). It provides general lighting of the stage from above and in front of the performers.	It helps the audience see what is happening on stage. It prevents performers or the audience from being blinded by the light. It is the most often used angle of lighting.
b	Backlight		
c	Up-light		
d	Sidelight		

Gels, barn doors and gobos

Guided

1   Write a definition for each of the stage lighting accessories below.

> Think about how each item is used. Include this information as part of your definitions.

(a) A gel: A gel is a sheet of coloured plastic that is placed in front of a lamp (using a gel holder) in order to change the colour of the light produced.

(b) A colour changer: ....

....

....

(c) A barn door: ....

....

....

(d) A gobo: ....

....

....

2   What type of gobo could you use to represent the following locations, times or seasons?

(a) Prison: ....

(b) Tropical island: ....

(c) Woodland: ....

(d) Church: ....

(e) Night-time: ....

(f) Winter: ....

3   Read through the outline of a play below. How could you use lighting accessories to highlight some of the main elements of the story for an audience?

> Berlin, 1961. The Berlin Wall separates two lovers. They invent different methods of getting messages to each other and plan to be together, but are constantly frustrated by the physical barrier of the wall.

....

....

....

....

....

....

....

....

....

....

Structure and focus

> **Guided**

1 The definitions below describe different lighting techniques. Tick (✓) to show which of the definitions are true and which are false.

For the definitions you decide are false, make sure you can describe the lighting technique correctly.

	Term and definition	True (✓)	False (✓)
a	**State:** How the lights are being used and the overall effect produced at any one time during the performance.	✓	
b	**Blackout:** When there is a total power failure, resulting in the performance not being able to continue.		
c	**Cue:** This is the signifier to show when the next lighting state should take place. Cues may be physical (such as the entrance / exit of a character) or verbal / audible (such as a performer saying a specific line or a sound effect).		
d	**Snap:** This is where two lighting effects are exactly the same.		
e	**Fade:** This is where light comes in or out gradually. The exact amount of time can be decided in advance and programmed into a lighting desk.		
f	**Cross fade:** Similar to a fade, but this is where one lighting state is gradually taken out to be replaced by another lighting state gradually fading in.		

2 Which lighting techniques could you use to support the following structural elements of a performance?

(a) The end of the performance: ....

(b) A split scene: ....

(c) A performer suddenly addressing an audience directly: ....

3 Read the scenario below. Explain which lighting techniques you would use to enhance the scene for an audience.

A split scene. On one side of the stage a man calmly explains to his superior officer that he is 'encouraging' a prisoner to provide him with information on others. On the other side of the stage, it becomes clear that this 'encouragement' takes the form of violent and brutal torture. The focus switches between the two scenes several times.

....

....

....

....

....

....

....

....

....

....

The set designer

> **Guided**

1 Complete the sentences below to describe the role of the set designer. Use words from the box.

consistency	~~physical~~	levels	entrances
exits	realised	messages	director

A set designer creates the physical location on stage. This conveys setting, and key themes and

...................., to the audience. A set designer works with the .... to establish what

the set should communicate and to ensure there is .... with other design elements.

They develop initial ideas to create an appropriate space, including a range of .... and

...................., and possibly different .... They then work with the construction team

to ensure the set is .... as practically and as closely as possible to the original design.

2 Complete the table to show which tasks are the primary responsibilities of the director and
which are the primary responsibilities of the set designer. Use a tick (✓) to show your answers.

> When staging a production, tasks will be shared out so sometimes the responsibility may not always rest
> with just one person. Here, think about who is **primarily** responsible for the completion of the task.

Task	Primary responsibility of	
	the director (✓)	the set designer (✓)
Working with members of the construction crew to build and realise a set that reflects the intended design		
Producing final set designs		
Organising the rehearsal schedule		
Representing the themes and issues of the play through the set		

3 Read the extract below.

> ELIZABETH: This is your mess. I want nothing more to do with it. [*Exits*]
>
> [KAREN *is left, staring at the box fearfully. She looks around to ensure she is alone and moves to check
> there is no one at the door. She moves back to the box and picks it up. She then takes the box and exits.*]

The director has given you the following information: 'The performance is set in 1862 and is
naturalistic. Elizabeth and Karen are both young servant girls in a large townhouse belonging to
a wealthy family. The room is a spare bedroom with very little furniture.'

As a set designer, discuss how you would use the set to bring this extract to life for your audience.

....

....

....

....

....

....

....

....

Had a go ☐   Nearly there ☐   Nailed it! ☐

Style and genre

> **Guided**

1   Look at Figures 1 and 2 below. For each one, identify the style of set design, and explain your decision.

> In your explanations, try to refer to specific details in each photograph.

(a)   Style: Naturalistic

How I can tell:

....

....

....

....

....

Figure 1 Almeida Theatre, Headlong & Nottingham Playhouse co-production of *1984*

(b)   Style: Abstract

How I can tell:

....

....

....

....

....

....

....

Figure 2 RSC production of *Twelfth Night*, 1997

2   As a set designer, you are working with a director who has decided that the style of a production will be physical theatre, where the performers will climb the walls and hang from the ceiling.

Describe the practical considerations you would have to take into account when designing a set for this style of production.

> Remember: a set needs to be practical for the performers to be able to work with it in performance.

....

....

....

....

....

....

....

....

Colours, location and time

Guided 1 Read the scene descriptions below. For each scene, explain what colours you would mainly use in the set design to help emphasise the physical location, as well as the mood and atmosphere.

> Think carefully about the audience. What is the mood and atmosphere you need to convey?

(a) | An orchard, where two lovers meet in secret. In one corner, under a tree, is a bench. |

To emphasise the location as an orchard, I would mainly use brown and green to indicate a large number of trees. To reflect the emotions of the lovers and the fact that they risk being caught, I would paint the bench upon which they sit red, symbolising the love and passion they have for each other, as well as the danger they may be in.

(b) | A simple chapel belonging to a late 17th-century agricultural community. |

....

....

....

....

....

....

(c) | The luxurious office of a corrupt town mayor in the early 19th century. |

....

....

....

....

....

....

....

2 Consider the locations and items of stage furniture below. Make notes on how you could represent the time period indicated in each case through the set.

> Think carefully about the materials and styles that would have been used in each time period.

Locations:

(a) A dining room in 1600: ....

....

(b) A dining room in 1912: ....

....

Stage furniture:

(c) A rustic dining table in 1692: ....

....

(d) A dining table in 2008: ....

....

Practicality, health and safety

> Guided

1 List **six** aspects you would need to consider in order to design and construct a practical set for a touring production. Give a reason for each of your answers.

	Practical aspect of set to consider	Reasons
a	Use of space	It should be simple for a performer to reach different parts of the performance area quickly and safely.
b		
c		
d		
e		
f		

2 Read the situations involving set below. For each situation, suggest the possible health and safety hazards and how, as a set designer, you could resolve them.

> Think carefully about how a performer needs to move on stage and around the set. What are the potential hazards for the cast, crew and audience?

	Situation	Potential hazards	Possible solutions
a	Two performers, engaged in a fight, must chase each other across the stage, climbing a spiral staircase to a balcony.		
b	Candles are used to represent a specific era. These are placed on top of a wooden table.		
c	A large, rustic wooden table is used in Act 2 of a four-act play. It needs to be brought on and then removed during the scene changes.		

Props and stage furniture

Guided

1 Look through the items listed in the table below. For each, tick (✓) to show whether it is a personal prop, stage furniture or scenery.

	Item	Personal prop (✓)	Stage furniture (✓)	Scenery (✓)
a	Stage flat			✓
b	Handkerchief			
c	Mobile phone			
d	Table			
e	Landline telephone			
f	Umbrella			
g	Staircase			
h	Desk lamp			

2 Consider the characters below. What props could you use to communicate key information about them to an audience?

Remember to think carefully about aspects such as the time period as well as the character's status.

(a)   A young woman who works in an industrial canteen, in the present day.

....

....

....

(b)   A young woman studying in a library in the late 19th century.

....

....

....

(c)   A duke from the early 17th century.

....

....

....

(d)   A doctor in an early 19th-century Russian town.

....

....

....

Levels, entrances and exits

> **Guided**

1 Complete the table below about what levels can convey to an audience.

	Levels can convey	Reason
a	Power	If a character is raised above others, the levels could show that this character has more power than the others. Alternatively, if a character is placed lower than others, it may show they have less power than those placed above them.
b		
c		
d		

2 Imagine there is an entrance/exit in each of the stage positions below. Suggest how each entrance/exit might be used for effect.

> Think about the audience.

(a)

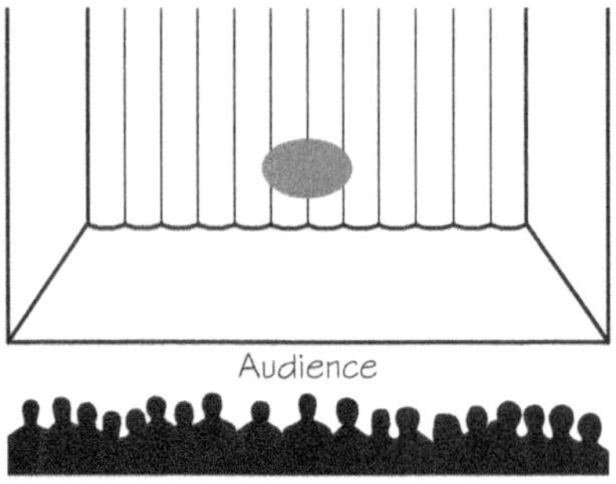

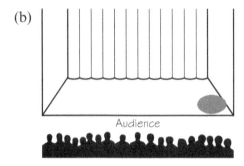

Audience

Figure 1

Upstage centre (USC): ....
....
....
....

(b)

Audience

Figure 2

Downstage left (DSL): ....
....
....
....

(c)

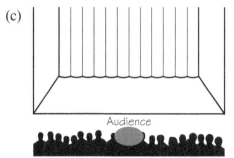

Audience

Figure 3

Through the audience: ....
....
....
....

Types of staging and terminology

⟩ **Guided** ⟩ 1 Look at Figure 1 below. Specific areas of the stage have been marked A–D. Identify each
   position on stage using the correct terminology.

> Remember that with stage positions, left and right are always from the perspective of the performer
> and not the audience.

A: Downstage centre

B: ....

C: ....

D: ....

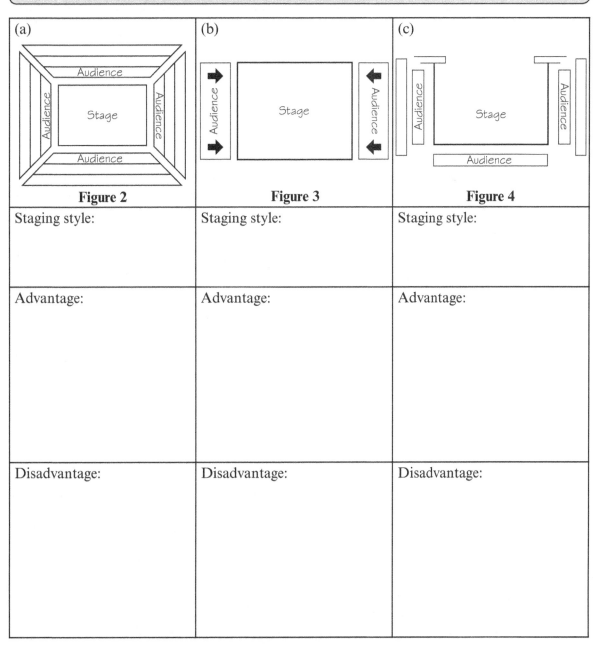

Figure 1

2 Look at Figures 2–4 below, showing different staging types. For each, identify the type of staging
   and then describe **one** advantage and **one** disadvantage of that staging style.

> When you consider the advantages and disadvantages of each staging type, make sure you think about
> the audience and how the staging type might affect their experience.

(a) **Figure 2**	(b) **Figure 3**	(c) **Figure 4**
Staging style:	Staging style:	Staging style:
Advantage:	Advantage:	Advantage:
Disadvantage:	Disadvantage:	Disadvantage:

Symbolism, semiotics, spatial consideration and depth

⟩ Guided ⟩ 1   Read the following scenario.

> A young woman suffers from an eating disorder. For many years, her family have tried to find her the correct support she needs to be treated. However, they keep finding themselves frustrated and not able to make the progress they want or need.

(a)   Write a short paragraph to describe how you would use set to symbolise the key theme in the scenario.

I would have a series of patterned curtains at the back of the stage, which could be drawn at the start of each scene and used to represent different locations – for example, comfortable curtains for home and clinical curtains for the hospital. Each curtain could include symbolic patterns, such as the outline of a wall for frustration, indicating that the characters are constantly trying to break down barriers.

(b)   Describe how you could use semiotics to convey this situation to an audience.

....

....

....

....

....

2   Now read through the scene outline below, which is for the above scenario.

> Scene: The young woman and her mother attend an appointment with a doctor, who reveals that there has been a mistake and that the young woman will not be receiving the psychiatric support she needs and was promised.

(a)   Sketch a plan of the set for this scene, focusing on spatial consideration. Annotate the sketch to explain your ideas.

> Think about the space the performers need to work and where they can stand.

(b)   Write a short paragraph to suggest how you could use depth for effect in the same scene above.

....

....

....

....

....

The sound designer

Guided 1 Complete the sentences below about the role of the sound designer. Use words from the box.

locations	music	~~sound effects~~	editing
technicians	emotions	time periods	musicians

A sound designer designs the sound effects and .... for a production. They work

with the director to create a sound design that reflects the chosen style and helps to communicate

key ideas, themes and .... to an audience, as well as .... and ....

The sound designer will read the text to understand exactly what is required from the sound (for

example, what music is needed, and why). Initial ideas are developed into a final design. The

sound designer may then work with .... and .... to supervise the recording,

.... and production of the sound effects and/or music.

2 Complete the following table to show which tasks are the primary responsibilities of the director and which are the primary responsibilities of the sound designer. Use a tick (✓) to show your answer.

> When staging a production, tasks will be shared out so sometimes the responsibility may not always rest with just one person. Here, think about who is **primarily** responsible for the completion of the task.

Task	Primary responsibility of	
	the director (✓)	the sound designer (✓)
Working with a team of designers to create a consistent design approach for the overall production		
Producing final sound designs		
Representing the themes and issues of the play through the sound and music		
Working with the production crew to prepare sound effects for the final performance		

3 Read the extract below.

> ELIZABETH: This is your mess. I want nothing more to do with it. [*Exits*]
>
> [KAREN *is left, staring at the box fearfully. She looks around to ensure she is alone and moves to check there is no one at the door. She moves back to the box and picks it up. She then takes the box and exits.*]

You are designing the sound for this production. The director has given you the following
information: 'Set in 1862, the performance is naturalistic. Elizabeth and Karen are young servant
girls in the large townhouse of a wealthy family. It is late at night; the atmosphere is eerie.'

As a sound designer, discuss how you would use sound to bring this extract to life for your audience.

....

....

....

....

....

....

....

Music and sound effects

> **Guided**

1 List **three** advantages and **three** disadvantages of using live sound and/or live music in a performance.

(a) Advantages:

(i) The sound effects/music could be fully integrated into the performance, blending in smoothly and adapting to the performer's specific performance that day/the live action on stage.

(ii) ....

....

....

(iii) ....

....

....

(b) Disadvantages:

(i) ....

....

....

(ii) ....

....

....

(iii) ....

....

....

2 Read the scenarios below. What sound effects could you use to help convey the required information to an audience? For each scenario, write a short paragraph describing your ideas.

> Think carefully about the detail of what is happening in each scenario. What would an audience need to understand in each case? Remember that sound effects can provide essential information when action is happening off stage, and a strong context when it is taking place on stage.

(a) | A man is taken away and executed by hanging. The action takes place off stage. |

....

....

....

....

(b) | A man is on hold on the telephone, waiting to receive some important information. His family wait, anxious and full of anticipation. The action takes place on stage. |

....

....

....

....

Atmosphere and time

⟩ **Guided** ⟩   1   Look at the types of atmosphere listed in the table below. How could you use music or sound effects to convey each atmosphere? Note your ideas in the table.

	Atmosphere	Sound effects	Music
a	Fear-filled	Heartbeat, gradually getting quicker. Creaking doors opening. Sudden scream.	Quiet, sustained music that builds up to a crescendo. Low-pitched notes played on stringed instruments.
b	Joyous		
c	Comic		

2   Consider the following scenarios. For each one, write a short paragraph to describe how you could convey the time period and atmosphere of the scene to an audience using either sound effects or music.

> Look out for information that tells you about the time period in which the scenario is set. Think carefully about how you will use sound effects and music to help establish that time period, as well as an appropriate atmosphere for the audience.

(a)   A busy street in an early 16th-century town.

....
....
....
....
....

(b)   A busy street in a 21st-century town.

....
....
....
....
....

(c)   A 1980s torture chamber in a military-run state where political prisoners are interrogated.

....
....
....
....
....

Location and genre

Guided 1 Match the locations listed below to the sound effects that could be used to represent them.

Docks	Wind blowing in the trees. Birdsong.
An orchard	Children laughing. Sound effect of a football being kicked.
A workplace canteen	Seagulls crying. The sound effect of the sea.
A playground	Quiet hum of people talking. Crockery being knocked together.

2 Look at the genres below. As a sound designer, what key features would you look for in a piece of music to be used in a play of each genre? Make notes about your ideas.

> Remember that genre refers to the type or category of theatre. As a sound designer, you might also need to think about style (the way a piece of theatre is performed, such as expressionism) and whether the production is naturalistic or abstract.

(a) Historical drama: ....

....

....

....

(b) Romantic comedy: ....

....

....

....

(c) Political drama: ....

....

....

....

3 Describe how you would use music or sound effects to reflect the genre of your performance text.

Genre of performance text: ....

....

....

....

....

....

....

Sound equipment and levels

Guided

1 Look at the images of sound equipment in the table below. Identify each piece of equipment and then add notes to explain how it can be used in sound design and production.

a	Figure 1	Equipment: Laptop How it can be used: Can be used to edit, store and play music and sound effects.
b	Figure 2	Equipment: How it can be used:
c	Figure 3	Equipment: How it can be used:
d	Figure 4	Equipment: How it can be used:
e	Figure 5	Equipment: How it can be used:
f	Figure 6	Equipment: How it can be used:

To make sure the sound design has the desired impact on the audience, it is important to consider volume. Is the volume of sound effects and/or music appropriate?

2 Give **one** possible consequence of the music being too loud in a performance.

....

....

3 Give **one** possible consequence of the music being too quiet in a performance.

....

....

4 Briefly describe how you could position speakers for effect.

....

....

1984: overview

Only revise pages 68 and 69 if *1984* is your performance text.

Only revise pages 68 and 69 if *1984* is your performance text.

> **Guided**

1 Decide which of these statements about *1984* are true and which are false. Use a tick (✓) to show your answers.

You need to know about the **context** in which the text was created and performed. For the statements you decide are false, make sure you know the correct answer.

	Statement	True	False
a	*1984* was adapted by Robert Icke and Duncan Macmillan from the novel by George Orwell.	✓	
b	It was first performed in 2013.		
c	The first performance took place in Liverpool.		
d	The play is set in Oceania.		
e	The play is set in 1984.		
f	The play takes the state versus the individual as a central theme.		
g	The play ends with Winston escaping from his detention.		
h	The play is structured into two acts.		

2 During the opening section of the play, Winston is surrounded by the Company. Imagine you are directing this section. Explain how you would use staging to convey the way the two different time periods come together.

Staging refers to the deliberate choices you make about where the performers stand and how they move on stage to communicate character, relationships and plot to the audience. It is also about how you create interesting stage pictures using the combination of design elements such as set, props and lighting.

....

....

....

....

....

....

3 Choose a scene (or scenes) from *1984*. Complete these director's notes relating to **two** themes you want to convey to an audience.

Directors often give titles to scenes, even if there are no scene titles in the text. This helps to describe the scenes to performers and to plan rehearsals.

Play: *1984*	
Scene:	
Scene title:	
Theme 1:	**Theme 2:**
Ideas for establishing theme 1:	**Ideas for establishing theme 2:**

1984: plot

> **Guided**

1 Put these key moments into the order in which they appear in the play.

> The sections referred to here have been created to help you navigate around the play.

Winston is tortured until he eventually betrays Julia.	Opening section
Winston and Julia meet O'Brien, who claims to be part of the resistance movement. They agree to join the fight against Big Brother.	Middle section 1
Julia passes Winston a note and they agree to meet in the countryside, where they begin their love affair.	Middle section 2
A child from next door screams out loud that Winston is a Thought Criminal.	Closing section

2 Answer the following questions about the events from the **opening section**.

> Put your answers into the correct **context** to help you understand character motive and plot development.

(a) Who does the Voice claim Winston is writing the book for?

....

(b) Why does Winston appear confused throughout the opening section?

....

....

3 Answer the following questions about the events from **middle section 1**.

(a) What does Symes refer to as a 'beautiful thing'?

....

(b) How does Winston feel about destroying the photograph that proves three men are innocent?

....

....

4 Answer the following questions about the events from **middle section 2**.

(a) What is the name of the resistance organisation?

....

(b) Why is O'Brien so calm and patient with Winston during the torture?

....

....

5 Answer the following questions about the events from the **closing section**.

(a) At what point does the Host claim the Party fell?

....

(b) Imagine you are producing *1984*. In no more than 40 words, write a description of the production to be used in an online advertisement through social media.

....

....

An Inspector Calls: overview

> Only revise pages 70 and 71 if *An Inspector Calls* is your performance text.

> **Guided**

1   Decide which of these statements about *An Inspector Calls* are true and which are false. Use a tick (✓) to show your answers.

> You need to know about the **context** in which the text was created and performed. For the statements you decide are false, make sure you know the correct answer.

	Statement	True	False
a	*An Inspector Calls* was written by J.B. Priestley.	✓	
b	It was first performed in 1945.		
c	The first performance took place in London.		
d	The play is set in the fictional town of Brumley.		
e	The play is set in 1914, just before the outbreak of the First World War.		
f	The play takes social responsibility as a central theme.		
g	Inspector Goole claims that Eva Smith and Daisy Renton are the same person.		
h	The play is structured into five acts.		

2   In Act 2, Inspector Goole questions Gerald. Sheila is also in the room and there is a heated exchange between the young couple. Imagine you are directing this section. Explain how you would use staging to convey the changing relationships in this scene.

> **Staging** refers to the deliberate choices you make about where the performers stand and how they move on stage to communicate character, relationships and plot to the audience. It is also about how you create interesting stage pictures using the combination of design elements such as set, props and lighting.

....

....

....

....

....

....

3   Choose a scene (or scenes) from *An Inspector Calls*. Complete these director's notes relating to **two** of the themes you want to convey to an audience.

Play: *An Inspector Calls* **Scene:** **Scene title:**	
	Giving titles to scenes helps to describe the scenes to performers and to plan rehearsals.

Theme 1:	Theme 2:
Ideas for establishing theme 1:	**Ideas for establishing theme 2:**

An Inspector Calls: plot

Guided

1 Put these key moments into the order in which they appear in the play.

> Through hard questioning, Mrs Birling admits the girl came to her for money but she refused to help her.

> Gerald returns and indicates that he does not think Inspector Goole is a real police officer and that the family have been deceived.

> The Birlings are celebrating the engagement of their daughter, Sheila, to Gerald Croft. A mysterious Inspector arrives to question them about the death of a young woman.

Act 1

Act 2

Act 3

2 Answer the following questions about the events from **Act 1**.

> Make sure you are able to put the answers into the correct **context** of the play. This will help your understanding of character motive and plot development.

(a) In which location does Act 1 take place?

....

(b) What occasion are the family celebrating?

....

(c) Why does Gerald continually agree with Mr Birling during the opening section of Act 1?

....

....

3 Answer the following questions about the events from **Act 2**.

(a) What does Gerald believe the girl's name to be?

....

(b) In which month did the affair between Gerald and Daisy end?

....

(c) Why does Sheila try to stop Mrs Birling from standing up to the Inspector?

....

....

4 Answer the following questions about the events from **Act 3**.

(a) Who does Inspector Goole accuse of starting the whole process off?

....

(b) How does Mr Birling confirm that Inspector Goole is not a police officer?

....

(c) Imagine you are producing *An Inspector Calls*. In no more than 40 words, write a description of the production to be used in an online advertisement through social media.

....

....

Blue Stockings: overview

Only revise pages 72 and 73 if *Blue Stockings* is your performance text.

Guided ▷   1   Decide which of these statements about *Blue Stockings* are true and which are false. Use a tick (✓) to show your answers.

> You need to know about the **context** in which the text was created and performed. For the statements you decide are false, make sure you know the correct answer.

	Statement	True	False
a	*Blue Stockings* was written by Jessica Swale.	✓	
b	It was first performed in 2013.		
c	The first professional performance took place at Shakespeare's Globe.		
d	The play is set in Cambridge.		
e	The play is set in 1986.		
f	The play takes equality and protest as central themes.		
g	The women are granted the right to graduate at the end of the play.		
h	The play is structured into three acts.		

2   In Act 1, Scene 13, Mrs Welsh makes a passionate speech in support of graduation for women. Simultaneously, Maeve leaves for personal reasons. Imagine you are directing this section. Explain how you would use staging to convey the different locations in this split scene.

> **Staging** refers to the deliberate choices you make about where the performers stand and how they move on stage to communicate character, relationships and plot to the audience. It is also about how you create interesting stage pictures using the combination of design elements such as set, props and lighting.

....

....

....

....

....

....

3   Choose a scene (or scenes) from *Blue Stockings*. Complete these director's notes relating to **two** of the themes you want to convey to an audience.

Play: *Blue Stockings* **Scene:** **Scene title:**	Giving titles to scenes helps to describe the scenes to performers and to plan rehearsals.
Theme 1:	**Theme 2:**
Ideas for establishing theme 1:	**Ideas for establishing theme 2:**

Blue Stockings: plot

> Guided

1 Put these key moments into the order in which they appear in the play.

During the vote, there is a violent protest against women being allowed to graduate. The vote is lost.	Act 1, Scene 4
Tess and Carolyn meet Holmes and Lloyd in a shop. Lloyd is unable to contain his disgust that women are being educated and launches into a vicious tirade against them.	Act 1, Scene 8
The students gather to listen to a lecture from renowned scientist, Dr Maudsley.	Act 2, Scene 6
Tess and Will meet in Tess's room. Will tries to warn Tess about her reputation. They argue and Will leaves.	Act 2, Scene 11

2 Answer the following questions about the events from **Act 1, Prologue** to **Scene 7**.

> Put your answers into the correct **context** to help you understand character motive and plot development.

(a) What is the subject of Dr Maudsley's lecture?

....

(b) Why is Tess so angry about being told to leave the lecture?

....

....

3 Answer the following questions about the events from **Act 1, Scenes 8–13**.

(a) How does Carolyn define the difference between science and the arts?

....

(b) Why does Mrs Welsh try to distance herself from the Suffragettes?

....

....

4 Answer the following questions about the events from **Act 2, Scenes 1–6**.

(a) Where is Carolyn trying to escape to in disguise?

....

(b) Why does Lloyd get so angry about women gaining an education?

....

....

5 Answer the following questions about the events from **Act 2, Scenes 7–12**.

(a) How are the women tested at the end of their course?

....

(b) Imagine you are producing *Blue Stockings*. In no more than 40 words, write a description of the production to be used in an online advertisement through social media.

....

....

The Crucible: overview

> Only revise pages 74 and 75 if *The Crucible* is your performance text.

Guided   1   Decide which of these statements about *The Crucible* are true and which are false. Use a tick (✓) to show your answers.

> You need to know about the **context** in which the text was created and performed. For the statements you decide are false, make sure you know the correct answer.

	Statement	True	False
a	*The Crucible* was written by Arthur Miller.	✓	
b	It was first performed in 1953.		
c	The first performance took place in New Orleans, USA.		
d	The play is set in 1269.		
e	The story relates to the Salem witch trials.		
f	The play is a political metaphor for the McCarthy trials, which took place in the 1950s.		
g	Everyone who is accused of witchcraft in the play is definitely guilty.		
h	The play is structured into three acts.		

2   In Act 2, Elizabeth Proctor is arrested in her home in front of a large group. Imagine you are directing this section. Explain how you would use staging to show the relationships and tension between the characters.

> **Staging** refers to the deliberate choices you make about where the performers stand and how they move on stage to communicate character, relationships and plot to the audience. It is also about how you create interesting stage pictures using the combination of design elements such as set, props and lighting.

....

....

....

....

....

....

3   Choose a scene (or scenes) from *The Crucible*. Complete these director's notes about **two** themes you want to convey to the audience in this scene.

Play: *The Crucible*	
Scene:	Giving titles to scenes helps to describe the scenes to performers and to plan rehearsals.
Scene title:	
Theme 1:	**Theme 2:**
Ideas for establishing theme 1:	**Ideas for establishing theme 2:**

The Crucible: plot

Guided > **1** Put these key moments into the order in which they appear in the play.

| John Proctor confesses, then destroys his statement and is hanged. |
| In court, Elizabeth denies that Proctor and Abigail had an affair, unknowingly supporting Abigail rather than her husband. |
| Tituba confesses to witchcraft and names several women who she also claims work for the Devil. |
| Reverend Hale questions Proctor and Elizabeth about their Christian beliefs. |

Act 1
Act 2
Act 3
Act 4

2 Answer the following questions about the events from **Act 1**.

> Make sure you are able to put the answers into the correct **context** of the play. This will help your understanding of character motive and plot development.

(a) What are the names of the two girls who are taken ill?

....

(b) Why does Abigail blame Tituba for the witchcraft?

....

....

3 Answer the following questions about the events from **Act 2**.

(a) What item is discovered and considered proof that Elizabeth is a witch?

....

(b) Why is Mary so frightened to tell the truth that the girls are lying?

....

....

4 Answer the following questions about the events from **Act 3**.

(a) What does Proctor admit to the Court?

....

(b) How does Abigail feel when Mary accuses Proctor of witchcraft?

....

....

5 Answer the following questions about the events from **Act 4**.

(a) What does Reverend Parris tell Danforth he has found on his door?

....

(b) Why does Proctor withdraw his confession and rip up the statement?

....

....

DNA: overview

Only revise pages 76 and 77 if *DNA* is your performance text.

> **Guided**

1 Decide which of these statements about *DNA* are true and which are false. Use a tick (✓) to show your answers.

You need to know about the **context** in which the text was created and performed. For the statements you decide are false, make sure you know the correct answer.

	Statement	True	False
a	*DNA* was written by Dennis Kelly.	✓	
b	It was first performed professionally in 2008.		
c	The first performance took place in Glasgow.		
d	The play is set in Cardiff.		
e	The play is set in the 20th century.		
f	The play takes bullying as a central theme.		
g	The play ends with Adam being reunited with his family.		
h	The play is structured into two acts.		

2 During the opening section, Richard tries to stand up to John Tate. Imagine you are directing this section. Explain how you would use staging to convey the status conflict between the two characters.

Staging refers to the deliberate choices you make about where the performers stand and how they move on stage to communicate character, relationships and plot to the audience. It is also about how you create interesting stage pictures using the combination of design elements such as set, props and lighting.

....
....
....
....
....
....

3 Choose a scene (or scenes) from *DNA*. Complete these director's notes relating to **two** of the themes you want to convey to an audience.

Play: *DNA*	Giving titles to scenes helps to describe the scenes to performers and to plan rehearsals.
Scene:	
Scene title:	

Theme 1:	**Theme 2:**
Ideas for establishing theme 1:	**Ideas for establishing theme 2:**

DNA: plot

> **Guided**

1 Put these key moments into the order in which they appear in the play.

Richard meets Brian alone in a field. He outlines the impact the events have had on everyone in the group.

Weeks later, Adam is found alive. It is established that he has been living rough in a hedge.

Phil outlines his plan to cover up the death of Adam, giving everyone in the group specific instructions.

A man is arrested for the abduction of Adam. His DNA matches the jumper, as Cathy has taken a jumper from a man fitting the description given to the police.

Section 1

Section 2

Section 3

Section 4

2 Answer the following questions about the events from **Section 1**.

> Put your answers into the correct **context** to help you understand character motive and plot development.

(a) Why does Phil tell Danny to enter the woods with Jan on his back?

....

(b) How could you describe Leah, and what causes her to talk non-stop to Phil?

....

....

3 Answer the following questions about the events from **Section 2**.

(a) What does Phil threaten Brian with if he won't go to the police station?

....

(b) Why are the characters confused that someone has been arrested?

....

....

4 Answer the following questions about the events from **Section 3**.

(a) Where did Cathy find Adam?

....

(b) Why do Phil and Cathy encourage Brian to take part in killing Adam?

....

....

5 Answer the following questions about the events from **Section 4**.

(a) How has Brian's condition developed?

....

(b) Imagine you are producing *DNA*. In no more than 40 words, write a description of the production to be used in an online advertisement through social media.

....

....

Dr Korczak's Example: overview

Only revise pages 78 and 79 if *Dr Korczak's Example* is your performance text.

> **Guided**

1 Decide which of these statements about *Dr Korczak's Example* are true and which are false. Use a tick (✓) to show your answers.

You need to know about the **context** in which the text was created and performed. For the statements you decide are false, make sure you know the correct answer.

	Statement	True	False
a	*Dr Korczak's Example* was written by David Greig.	✓	
b	It was first performed in 2004.		
c	The first performance took place in London.		
d	The play is set in the Warsaw Ghetto.		
e	The play is set in 1916, during the First World War.		
f	The play takes social responsibility and respect of children as central themes.		
g	Dr Korczak protects and feeds approximately 200 children.		
h	The play is structured into three acts.		

2 In Scene 14, Dr Korczak visits Adam Cerniakov, concerned that the Nazis will send the children to the concentration camps. Imagine you are directing this section. Explain how you would use staging to convey the tension in this scene.

Staging refers to the deliberate choices you make about where the performers stand and how they move on stage to communicate character, relationships and plot to the audience. It is also about how you create interesting stage pictures using the combination of design elements such as set, props and lighting.

....

....

....

....

....

....

3 Choose a scene (or scenes) from *Dr Korczak's Example*. Complete these director's notes relating to **two** of the themes you want to convey to an audience.

Play: *Dr Korczak's Example* **Scene:** **Scene title:**	Giving titles to scenes helps to describe the scenes to performers and to plan rehearsals.
Theme 1:	**Theme 2:**
Ideas for establishing theme 1:	**Ideas for establishing theme 2:**

Dr Korczak's Example: plot

> **Guided**

1 Put these key moments into the order in which they appear in the play.

Cerniakov, discovering that the children will be transported to the camps, is devastated and commits suicide.	Scene 4
Adzio and Stephanie, angry with the priest for not letting the children play in the church garden, throw stones at the church windows, breaking them.	Scene 9
Adzio is introduced to the orphanage and meets Dr Korczak.	Scene 18
Stepan, a Christian, offers Dr Korczak an escape from the ghetto. It would mean abandoning the children so Dr Korczak refuses.	Scene 21

2 Answer the following questions about the events from **Scenes 1–6**.

> Put your answers into the correct **context** to help you understand character motive and plot development.

(a) Where has Adzio been living before coming to the orphanage?

....

(b) Why is Adzio so aggressive and resistant to help?

....

....

3 Answer the following questions about the events in **Scenes 7–12**.

(a) What is Adzio's punishment?

....

(b) Why is Dr Korczak so angry with the German soldier?

....

....

4 Answer the following questions about the events in **Scenes 13–18**.

(a) What does Adzio call the priest?

....

(b) Why is the priest worried about letting the children use the church garden?

....

....

5 Answer the following questions about the events in **Scenes 19–25**.

(a) What will happen to anyone found in the ghetto after the deadline to report to the railway yards?

....

(b) Why does Dr Korczak refuse the opportunity to be released as he boarded the train?

....

....

Government Inspector: overview

Only revise pages 80 and 81 if *Government Inspector* is your performance text.

> **Guided**

1 Decide which of these statements about *Government Inspector* are true and which are false. Use a tick (✓) to show your answers.

You need to know about the **context** in which the text was created and performed. For the statements you decide are false, make sure you know the correct answer.

	Statement	True	False
a	*Government Inspector* was written by Nikolai Gogol.	✓	
b	It was first performed in 1836.		
c	The first performance took place in Berlin, Germany.		
d	The play is set in 17th-century Russia.		
e	The story takes a satirical look at political corruption.		
f	The central theme of the play is mistaken identity.		
g	The Mayor is the central character in the town.		
h	The play is structured into three acts.		

2 In Act 4, Scene 8, the shopkeepers demand to speak to Khlestakov. You are directing the scene. Explain how you would use staging to demonstrate the rising tension.

Staging refers to the deliberate choices you make about where the performers stand and how they move on stage to communicate character, relationships and plot to the audience. It is also about how you create interesting stage pictures using the combination of design elements such as set, props and lighting.

....

....

....

....

....

....

3 Choose a scene (or scenes) from *Government Inspector*. Complete these director's notes about **two** themes you want to convey to the audience in this scene.

Play: *Government Inspector* **Scene:** **Scene title:**	Giving titles to scenes helps to describe the scenes to performers and to plan rehearsals.
Theme 1:	**Theme 2:**
Ideas for establishing theme 1:	**Ideas for establishing theme 2:**

Government Inspector: plot

> **Guided**   1   Put these key moments into the order in which they appear in the play.

The Mayor and Khlestakov meet. The Mayor believes that Khlestakov is a Government Inspector.	Act 1
Khlestakov and Osip escape before the truth is discovered. The people realise they have been deceived.	Act 2
The Mayor, panicking because a Government Inspector has arrived, orders the officials of the town to clean everything up.	Act 3
The officials of the town are individually introduced to Khlestakov and nervously bribe him.	Act 4
Khlestakov is welcomed into the Mayor's house and meets Anna and Maria.	Act 5

2   Answer the following question about the events from **Act 1**.

> Make sure you are able to put the answers into the correct **context** of the play. This will help your understanding of character motive and plot development.

Why is the Mayor so stressed during the opening scene?

....

....

3   Answer the following question about the events from **Act 2**.

Why is Khlestakov so worried about the Mayor and other officials approaching his room?

....

....

4   Answer the following question about the events from **Act 3**.

Why do Anna and Maria constantly bicker throughout Act 3, Scene 1?

....

....

5   Answer the following question about the events from **Act 4**.

Why is Lyapkin-Tyapkin so nervous when meeting Khlestakov in Act 4, Scene 2?

....

....

6   Imagine you are producing *Government Inspector*. In no more than 40 words, write a description of the production to be used in an online advertisement through social media.

....

....

Twelfth Night: overview

> Only revise pages 82 and 83 if *Twelfth Night* is your performance text.

> Guided 1 Decide which of these statements about *Twelfth Night* are true and which are false. Use a tick (✓) to show your answers.

> You need to know about the **context** in which the text was created and performed. For the statements you decide are false, make sure you know the correct answer.

	Statement	True	False
a	*Twelfth Night* was written by Ben Jonson.		✓
b	It was first performed in the early 16th century.		
c	The first recorded performance took place in London c1601–1602.		
d	The play is set in Illyria (a fictional place).		
e	The title is a reference to the Festival of Midsummer.		
f	The play takes mistaken identity as a central theme.		
g	Malvolio is the character with the highest status and power in the play.		
h	The play is structured into five acts.		

2 In Act 2, Scene 5, Malvolio is tricked by the pranksters, who are hiding. You are directing the scene. Explain how you would use staging to make effective use of the asides.

> **Staging** refers to the deliberate choices you make about where the performers stand and how they move on stage to communicate character, relationships and plot to the audience. It is also about how you create interesting stage pictures using the combination of design elements such as set, props and lighting.

....

....

....

....

....

....

3 Choose a scene (or scenes) from *Twelfth Night*. Complete these director's notes about **two** themes you want to convey to the audience in this scene.

Play: *Twelfth Night* **Scene:** **Scene title:**	Giving titles to scenes helps to describe the scenes to performers and to plan rehearsals.
Theme 1:	**Theme 2:**
Ideas for establishing theme 1:	**Ideas for establishing theme 2:**

Twelfth Night: plot

> **Guided**

1   Put these key moments into the order in which they appear in the play.

Malvolio finds a letter, supposedly from Olivia, but actually it is a trick played on him by Sir Toby, Sir Andrew, Maria, Fabian and Feste.	Act 1
Viola and Sebastian are reunited and true identities are revealed. Olivia and Sebastian, Orsino and Viola, Sir Toby and Maria all get married.	Act 2
Viola is saved from a shipwreck and disguises herself as a man to gain employment with Orsino.	Act 3
Olivia mistakes Sebastian for Cesario, helping and caring for him – which is very confusing for Sebastian, as he has never met her before!	Act 4
Sir Andrew challenges Cesario (Viola) to a duel in an attempt to impress Olivia.	Act 5

2   Answer the following question about the events from **Act 1**.

> Make sure you are able to put the answers into the correct **context** of the play. This will help your understanding of character motive and plot development.

Why does Sir Toby want Sir Andrew to stay?

....

....

3   Answer the following questions about the events from **Act 2**.

Why do Maria, Sir Toby, Sir Andrew and Feste want to play a trick on Malvolio?

....

....

4   Answer the following questions about the events from **Act 3**.

Why is Olivia so confused by Malvolio's behaviour in Act 3, Scene 4?

....

....

5   Answer the following questions about the events from **Act 4**:

Why is Sebastian so confused when Olivia stops the fight between him and Sir Andrew and Sir Toby?

....

....

6   Answer the following question about the events in **Act 5**.

Imagine you are producing *Twelfth Night*. In no more than 40 words, write a description of the production to be used in an online advertisement through social media.

....

....

Timed test

SECTION A

Answer **ALL** questions that relate to the **ONE** performance text studied for examination purposes.

There are five questions in total for each performance text.

Text studied	Questions	Extract
1984 Prescribed edition: published by Oberon Plays, ISBN 9781783190614	Questions 1(a) to 1(c) Go to page 85	Near the end of the play from: 'We hear a VOICE as at the beginning of the play' to the end. **Prescribed edition**: from near the top of page 88 (8 lines from the top) to near the middle of page 90.
An Inspector Calls Prescribed edition: published by Heinemann, ISBN 9780435232825	Questions 2(a) to 2(c) Go to page 87	Act 3, from when the Inspector exits for the final time to where Eric responds to Mr Birling's threat to have Sheila leave the room by saying, 'That'll be terrible for her, won't it?' **Prescribed edition**: from the bottom of page 56 to near the top of page 59.
Blue Stockings Prescribed edition: published by Nick Hern Books, ISBN 9781848423299	Questions 3(a) to 3(c) Go to page 89	Act 2, Scene 3, from the beginning of the scene, to Scene 4, MRS WELSH 'No, it is not.' **Prescribed edition**: from near the top of page 79 to the middle of page 82.
The Crucible Prescribed edition: published by Methuen (student edition), ISBN 9781408108390	Questions 4(a) to 4(c) Go to page 91	Act 3, when Elizabeth is brought into the court, from DANFORTH 'Bring her out!' to DANFORTH 'She spoke nothing of lechery'. **Prescribed edition**: from halfway down page 101 to 6 lines from the bottom of page 103.
DNA Prescribed edition: published by Oberon Plays (school edition), ISBN 9781840029529	Questions 5(a) to 5(c) Go to page 93	Section 2, from the entrance of Phil, Leah, Lou and Danny in the wood to where Richard and Cathy enter. **Prescribed edition**: from the top of page 33 to near the top of page 36.
Dr Korczak's Example Prescribed edition: published by Capercaillie Books, ISBN 9780954520618	Questions 6(a) to 6(c) Go to page 95	Scenes 10 and 11, from when Stephanie enters carrying a clipboard to where Korczak bangs the gavel at the end of Scene 11. **Prescribed edition**: from near the bottom of page 36 to near the bottom of page 39.
Government Inspector Prescribed edition: published by Faber & Faber, ISBN 9780571280490	Questions 7(a) to 7(c) Go to page 97	Act 3, Scene 4, from the start of the scene to when Khlestakov claims to be the Commander-in-Chief. **Prescribed edition**: from page 57 to 7 lines from the bottom of page 59.
Twelfth Night Prescribed edition: published by New Longman Shakespeare, ISBN 9780582365780	Questions 8(a) to 8(c) Go to page 99	Act 2, Scene 4, lines 1–79, from the beginning of the scene to where Feste exits. **Prescribed edition**: from near the middle of page 65 to near the bottom of page 69.

SECTION B

Questions 9a and 9b – Answer **BOTH** questions in relation to **ONE** performance you have seen.	Go to page 101

SECTION A: BRINGING TEXTS TO LIFE
1984, George Orwell, Robert Icke and Duncan Macmillan
Answer ALL questions.

**You are involved in staging a production of this play. Use your copy of the performance text to
locate and read this extract from the play: near the end of the play from 'We hear a VOICE as at the
beginning of the play' to the end. If you have the prescribed edition of the text, this extract begins near
the top of page 88 (8 lines from the top) and ends near the middle of page 90.**

Make sure you:

- read each question carefully – for example, make sure you know exactly **how many** points you need to explain or how many suggestions you need to give

- identify and understand the command word for each question – for example, **explain** or **discuss**.

To answer these questions on *1984*, turn to page 102.

For Question (a):

- Make sure you refer to the **text** when making your decisions about the skills you want to include.

- Don't forget to consider any **stage directions** that may be included in the extract.

1 (a) There are specific choices in this extract for performers.

     (i) You are going to play the Host.
Explain **two** ways you would use
either **physical skills** or **vocal skills**
to play this character in this extract.

In the exam, the question will specify
whether you need to cover physical skills **or**
vocal skills. **You will not be given a choice.**
Make sure you are ready to answer either!

(4 marks)

     (ii) You are going to play Winston. He does not say anything throughout most of the scene,
although it is clear he can hear what is being said.

As a performer, give **three** suggestions of how you would use **performance skills** to
indicate Winston's thoughts and reactions throughout this extract.

You must provide a reason for each suggestion.   **(6 marks)**

  (b) There are specific choices in this extract for
a director.

For Question (b), you must remember to
refer to the **context** in which the text was
originally created and performed.

     (i) As a director, discuss how you would
use **one** of the **production elements below**
to bring this extract to life for your audience.

You should make reference to the context in which the text was created and performed.

Choose **one** of the following:

- costume
- sound
- set
- props/stage furniture
- lighting
- staging.   **(9 marks)**

In the exam, you will only be given a choice of **three** out of the six production elements listed above for this
question. You might get **any combination** of these options – so be prepared!

(ii) The Host is the one person who has all of the answers to the questions asked by the group.

As a director, discuss how the performer playing this role might demonstrate this to the audience in this extract and the complete play.

You must consider:

- voice
- physicality
- stage directions and stage space. **(12 marks)**

(c) There are specific choices in this extract for designers.

Discuss how you would use **one** design element to enhance the production of this extract for an audience.

> For Question (c), try to demonstrate **how** the selected design element would **improve** the performance for an audience.

Choose **one** of the following:

- costume
- lighting
- props/stage furniture
- set
- sound
- staging. **(14 marks)**

> In the exam, you will only be given a choice of **three** out of the six design elements listed above for this question. You might get **any combination** of these options – so be prepared!

(Total for Question 1 = 45 marks)

TOTAL FOR SECTION A = 45 MARKS

SECTION A: BRINGING TEXTS TO LIFE
An Inspector Calls, J.B. Priestley
Answer ALL questions.

You are involved in staging a production of this play. Use your copy of the performance text to locate and read this extract from the play: Act 3, from when the Inspector exits for the final time to where Eric responds to Mr Birling's threat to have Sheila leave the room by saying, 'That'll be terrible for her, won't it?' If you have the prescribed edition of the text, this extract begins at the top of page 57 and ends near the top of page 59.

Make sure you:

- read each question carefully – for example, make sure you know exactly **how many** points you need to explain or how many suggestions you need to give

- identify and understand the command word for each question – for example, **explain** or **discuss**.

To answer these questions on *An Inspector Calls*, turn to page 102.

For Question (a):

- Make sure you refer to the **text** when making your decisions about the skills you want to include.

- Don't forget to consider any **stage directions** that may be included in the extract.

---

2   (a)   There are specific choices in this extract for performers.

       (i)   You are going to play Mrs Birling. Explain **two** ways you would use either **physical skills** or **vocal skills** to play this character in this extract.

> In the exam, the question will specify whether you need to cover physical skills **or** vocal skills. **You will not be given a choice.** Make sure you are ready to answer either!

       (ii)   You are going to play Eric. He is feeling increasingly guilty about his part in Eva's downfall during this scene.

            As a performer, give **three** suggestions of how you would use **performance skills** to demonstrate Eric's feelings of guilt throughout this extract.

            You must provide a reason for each suggestion.   **(6 marks)**

   (b)   There are specific choices in this extract for a director.

> For Question (b), you must remember to refer to the **context** in which the text was originally created and performed.

       (i)   As a director, discuss how you would use **one** of the **production elements below** to bring this extract to life for your audience.

            You should make reference to the context in which the text was created and performed.

            Choose **one** of the following:

- costume
- set
- lighting
- sound
- props/stage furniture
- staging.   **(9 marks)**

In the exam, you will only be given a choice of **three** out of the six production elements listed above for this question. You might get **any combination** of these options – so be prepared!

(ii) Mr Birling is becoming increasingly angry and defensive.

As a director, discuss how the performer playing this role might demonstrate Mr Birling's reaction to the audience in this extract and the complete play.

You must consider:

- voice
- physicality
- stage directions and stage space.   **(12 marks)**

(c) There are specific choices in this extract for designers.

Discuss how you would use **one** design element to enhance the production of this extract for an audience.

> For Question (c), try to demonstrate **how** the selected design element would **improve** the performance for an audience.

Choose **one** of the following:

- costume
- lighting
- props/stage furniture

- set
- sound
- staging.   **(14 marks)**

> In the exam, you will only be given a choice of **three** out of the six design options elements above for this question. You might get **any combination** of these options – so be prepared!

(Total for Question 2 = 45 marks)

TOTAL FOR SECTION A = 45 MARKS

SECTION A: BRINGING TEXTS TO LIFE
Blue Stockings, Jessica Swale
Answer ALL questions.

You are involved in staging a production of this play. Use your copy of the performance text to locate and read this extract from the play: Act 2, Scene 3, from the beginning of the scene to Scene 4, MRS WELSH 'No, it is not.' If you have the prescribed edition of the text, this extract begins from near the top of page 79 to the middle of page 82.

> Make sure you:
> - read each question carefully – for example, make sure you know exactly **how many** points you need to explain or how many suggestions you need to give
> - identify and understand the command word for each question – for example, **explain** or **discuss**.
> **To answer these questions on *Blue Stockings*, turn to page 102.**

> For Question (a):
> - Make sure you refer to the **text** when making your decisions about the skills you want to include.
> - Don't forget to consider any **stage directions** that may be included in the extract.

3 (a) There are specific choices in this extract for performers.

   (i) You are going to play Mrs Welsh. Explain **two** ways you would use either **physical skills** or **vocal skills** to play this character in this extract.

> In the exam, the question will specify whether you need to cover physical skills **or** vocal skills. **You will not be given a choice.** Make sure you are ready to answer either!

(4 marks)

   (ii) You are going to play Tess. She is very much in love with Ralph and is trying to impress him with her knowledge while also trying to remain cool and calm. However, she is being swept away by her emotions.

   As a performer, give **three** suggestions of how you would use **performance skills** to show Tess's emotions throughout this extract.

   You must provide a reason for each suggestion.   **(6 marks)**

   (b) There are specific choices in this extract for a director.

> For Question (b), you must remember to refer to the **context** in which the text was originally created and performed.

   (i) As a director, discuss how you would use **one** of the **production elements below** to bring this extract to life for your audience.

   You should make reference to the context in which the text was created and performed.

   Choose **one** of the following:

   - costume   - set   - lighting
   - sound   - props/stage furniture   - staging.   **(9 marks)**

> In the exam, you will only be given a choice of **three** out of the six production elements listed above for this question. You might get **any combination** of these options – so be prepared!

(ii) Carolyn is desperate to attend the Suffragette meeting but is also keen to avoid getting Miss Blake into trouble.

As a director, discuss how the performer playing this role might demonstrate these conflicting emotions to the audience in this extract and the complete play.

You must consider:

- voice
- physicality
- stage directions and stage space.   **(12 marks)**

(c) There are specific choices in this extract for designers.

Discuss how you would use **one** design element to enhance the production of this extract for an audience.

> For Question (c), try to demonstrate **how** the selected design element would **improve** the performance for an audience.

Choose **one** of the following:

- costume
- lighting
- props/stage furniture
- set
- sound
- staging.   **(14 marks)**

> In the exam, you will only be given a choice of **three** out of the six design elements listed above for this question. You might get **any combination** of these options – so be prepared!

(Total for Question 3 = 45 marks)

TOTAL FOR SECTION A = 45 MARKS

SECTION A: BRINGING TEXTS TO LIFE
The Crucible, Arthur Miller
Answer ALL questions.

You are involved in staging a production of this play. Use your copy of the performance text to locate and read this extract from the play: Act 3, when Elizabeth is brought into the court, from DANFORTH 'Bring her out!' to DANFORTH 'She spoke nothing of lechery'. If you have the prescribed edition of the text, this extract begins halfway down page 101 and ends 6 lines from the bottom of page 103.

Make sure you:

- read each question carefully – for example, make sure you know exactly **how many** points you need to explain or how many suggestions you need to give
- identify and understand the command word for each question – for example, **explain** or **discuss**.

To answer these questions on *The Crucible*, turn to page 102.

For Question (a):

- Make sure you refer to the **text** when making your decisions about the skills you want to include.
- Don't forget to consider any **stage directions** that may be included in the extract.

---

4   (a)   There are specific choices in this extract for performers.

       (i)   You are going to play Elizabeth. Explain **two** ways you would use either **physical skills** or **vocal skills** to play this character in this extract.

> In the exam, the question will specify whether you need to cover physical skills **or** vocal skills. **You will not be given a choice.** Make sure you are ready to answer either!

(4 marks)

       (ii)   You are going to play Danforth. He is the judge with the highest status and most experience.

           As a performer, give **three** suggestions of how you would use **performance skills** to demonstrate his status from his entrance to the end of the extract.

           You must provide a reason for each suggestion.   **(6 marks)**

     (b)   There are specific choices in this extract for a director.

> For Question (b), you must remember to refer to the **context** in which the text was originally created and performed.

       (i)   As a director, discuss how you would use **one** of the **production elements below** to bring this extract to life for your audience.

           You should make reference to the context in which the text was created and performed.

           Choose **one** of the following:

- costume
- sound
- set
- props/stage furniture
- lighting
- staging.   **(9 marks)**

In the exam, you will only be given a choice of **three** out of the six production elements listed above for this question. You might get **any combination** of these options – so be prepared!

(ii) Proctor is the one person who can prove that the girls are frauds.

As a director, discuss how the performer playing this role might demonstrate this knowledge and responsibility to the audience in this extract and the complete play.

You must consider:

- voice
- physicality
- stage directions and stage space. **(12 marks)**

(c) There are specific choices in this extract for designers.

Discuss how you would use **one** design element to enhance the production of this extract for an audience.

> For Question (c), try to demonstrate **how** the selected design element would **improve** the performance for an audience.

Choose **one** of the following:

- costume
- lighting
- props/stage furniture
- set
- sound
- staging. **(14 marks)**

> In the exam, you will only be given a choice of **three** out of the six design elements listed above for this question. You might get **any combination** of these options – so be prepared!

(Total for Question 4 = 45 marks)

TOTAL FOR SECTION A = 45 MARKS

SECTION A: BRINGING TEXTS TO LIFE
DNA, Dennis Kelly
Answer ALL questions.

You are involved in staging a production of this play. Use your copy of the performance text to locate and read this extract from the play: Section 2, from the entrance of Phil, Leah, Lou and Danny in the Wood to where Richard and Cathy enter. If you have the prescribed edition of the text, this extract begins at the top of page 33 and ends near the top of page 36.

Make sure you:

- read each question carefully – for example, make sure you know exactly **how many** points you need to explain or how many suggestions you need to give

- identify and understand the command word for each question – for example, **explain** or **discuss**.

To answer these questions on *DNA*, turn to page 102.

For Question (a):

- Make sure you refer to the **text** when making your decisions about the skills you want to include.

- Don't forget to consider any **stage directions** that may be included in the extract.

---

5 (a)   There are specific choices in this extract for performers.

(i)   You are going to play Lou.
Explain **two** ways you would use
either **physical skills** or **vocal skills**
to play this character in this extract.

> In the exam, the question will specify whether you need to cover physical skills **or** vocal skills. **You will not be given a choice.** Make sure you are ready to answer either!

(4 marks)

(ii)   You are going to play Danny. He is panicking because he is terrified that he will not be able to get in to dental college.

As a performer, give **three** suggestions of how you would use **performance skills** to show Danny's fears throughout this extract.

You must provide a reason for each suggestion.   **(6 marks)**

(b)   There are specific choices in this extract for a director.

> For Question (b), you must remember to refer to the **context** in which the text was originally created and performed.

(i)   As a director, discuss how you would use **one** of the **production elements below** to bring this extract to life for your audience.

You should make reference to the context in which the text was created and performed.

Choose **one** of the following:

- costume
- set
- lighting
- sound
- props/stage furniture
- staging.   **(9 marks)**

In the exam, you will only be given a choice of **three** out of the six production elements listed above for this question. You might get **any combination** of these options – so be prepared!

(ii) Leah is the character who is shocked by the news that a man has been arrested and asks all of the important questions to discover what has happened.

As a director, discuss how the performer playing this role might demonstrate this to the audience in this extract and the complete play.

You must consider:

- voice
- physicality
- stage directions and stage space. **(12 marks)**

(c) There are specific choices in this extract for designers.

Discuss how you would use **one** design element to enhance the production of this extract for an audience.

> For Question (c), try to demonstrate **how** the selected design element would **improve** the performance for an audience.

Choose **one** of the following:

- costume
- lighting
- props/stage furniture
- set
- sound
- staging. **(14 marks)**

> In the exam, you will only be given a choice of **three** out of the six design elements listed above for this question. You might get **any combination** of these options – so be prepared!

(Total for Question 5 = 45 marks)

TOTAL FOR SECTION A = 45 MARKS

SECTION A: BRINGING TEXTS TO LIFE

Dr Korczak's Example, David Greig

Answer ALL questions.

You are involved in staging a production of this play. Use your copy of the performance text to locate and read this extract from the play: Scenes 10 and 11, from when Stephanie enters carrying a clipboard to where Korczak bangs the gavel at the end of Scene 11. If you have the prescribed edition of the text, this extract begins near the bottom of page 36 and ends near the bottom of page 39.

Make sure you:

- read each question carefully – for example, make sure you know exactly **how many** points you need to explain or how many suggestions you need to give
- identify and understand the command word for each question – for example, **explain** or **discuss**.

To answer these questions on *Dr Korczak's Example*, turn to page 102.

For Question (a):

- Make sure you refer to the **text** when making your decisions about the skills you want to include.
- Don't forget to consider any **stage directions** that may be included in the extract.

---

6 (a) There are specific choices in this extract for performers.

(i) You are going to play Stephanie.
Explain **two** ways you would use
either **physical skills** or **vocal skills**
to play this character in this extract.

> In the exam, the question will specify
> whether you need to cover physical skills **or**
> vocal skills. **You will not be given a choice.**
> Make sure you are ready to answer either!

(4 marks)

(ii) You are going to play Dr Korczak. He must give an air of leadership while also balancing this by giving authority to the children.

As a performer, give **three** suggestions of how you would use **performance skills** to show this balance throughout this extract.

You must provide a reason for each suggestion. **(6 marks)**

(b) There are specific choices in this extract for a director.

> For Question (b), you must remember to
> refer to the **context** in which the text was
> originally created and performed.

(i) As a director, discuss how you would use **one** of the **production elements below** to bring this extract to life for your audience.

You should make reference to the context in which the text was created and performed.

Choose **one** of the following:

- costume
- set
- lighting
- sound
- props/stage furniture
- staging. **(9 marks)**

In the exam, you will only be given a choice of **three** out of the six production elements listed above for this question. You might get **any combination** of these options – so be prepared!

(ii) Adzio constantly challenges Dr Korczak and tries to undermine the systems in place at the orphanage.

As a director, discuss how the performer playing the role of Adzio might demonstrate his behaviour towards Dr Korczak to the audience in this extract and the complete play.

You must consider:

- voice
- physicality
- stage directions and stage space. **(12 marks)**

(c) There are specific choices in this extract for designers.

Discuss how you would use **one** design element to enhance the production of this extract for an audience.

> For Question (c), try to demonstrate **how** the selected design element would **improve** the performance for an audience.

Choose **one** of the following:

- costume
- lighting
- props/stage furniture
- set
- sound
- staging. **(14 marks)**

> In the exam, you will only be given a choice of **three** out of the six design elements listed above for this question. You might get **any combination** of these options – so be prepared!

(Total for Question 6 = 45 marks)

TOTAL FOR SECTION A = 45 MARKS

SECTION A: BRINGING TEXTS TO LIFE
Government Inspector, Nikolai Gogol adapted by David Harrower
Answer ALL questions.

You are involved in staging a production of this play. Use your copy of the performance text to locate and read this extract from the play: Act 3, Scene 4, from the start of the scene to when Khlestakov claims to be the Commander-in-Chief. If you have the prescribed edition of the text, this extract begins on page 57 and ends 7 lines from the bottom of page 59.

Make sure you:

- read each question carefully – for example, make sure you know exactly **how many** points you need to explain or how many suggestions you need to give
- identify and understand the command word for each question – for example, **explain** or **discuss**.

To answer these questions on *Government Inspector*, turn to page 102.

For Question (a):

- Make sure you refer to the **text** when making your decisions about the skills you want to include.
- Don't forget to consider any **stage directions** that may be included in the extract.

7 (a) There are specific choices in this extract for performers.

    (i) You are going to play Anna.
Explain **two** ways you would use
either **physical skills** or **vocal skills**
to play this character in this extract.

In the exam, the question will specify whether you need to cover physical skills **or** vocal skills. **You will not be given a choice.** Make sure you are ready to answer either!

(4 marks)

    (ii) You are going to play Khlestakov. He enjoys telling his exaggerated stories to the captive audience of the town's citizens.

      As a performer, give **three** suggestions of how you would use **performance skills** to demonstrate the growing exaggeration in this extract.

      You must provide a reason for each suggestion.   **(6 marks)**

  (b) There are specific choices in this extract for a director.

For Question (b), you must remember to refer to the **context** in which the text was originally created and performed.

    (i) As a director, discuss how you would use **one** of the **production elements below** to bring this extract to life for your audience.

      You should make reference to the context in which the text was created and performed.

      Choose **one** of the following:

• costume	• set	• lighting
• sound	• props/stage furniture	• staging. **(9 marks)**

In the exam, you will only be given a choice of **three** out of the six production elements listed above for this question. You might get **any combination** of these options – so be prepared!

(ii) The Mayor only has one line in this extract, but has to watch and listen as Anna and Khlestakov flirt with each other.

As a director, discuss how the performer playing the role might demonstrate his reactions to the audience in this extract and the complete play.

You must consider:

- voice
- physicality
- stage directions and stage space. **(12 marks)**

(c) There are specific choices in this extract for designers.

Discuss how you would use **one** design element to enhance the production of this extract for an audience.

> For Question (c), try to demonstrate **how** the selected design element would **improve** the performance for an audience.

Choose **one** of the following:

- costume
- lighting
- props/stage furniture

- set
- sound
- staging. **(14 marks)**

> In the exam, you will only be given a choice of **three** out of the six design elements listed above for this question. You might get **any combination** of these options – so be prepared!

(Total for Question 7 = 45 marks)

TOTAL FOR SECTION A = 45 MARKS

SECTION A: BRINGING TEXTS TO LIFE
Twelfth Night, **William Shakespeare**
Answer ALL questions.

You are involved in staging a production of this play. Use your copy of the performance text to locate and read this extract from the play: Act 2, Scene 4, lines 1–79, from the beginning of the scene to where Feste exits. If you have the prescribed edition of the text, this extract begins near the middle of page 65 and ends near the bottom of page 69.

Make sure you:

- read each question carefully – for example, make sure you know exactly **how many** points you need to explain or how many suggestions you need to give

- identify and understand the command word for each question – for example, **explain** or **discuss**.

To answer these questions on *Twelfth Night*, turn to page 102.

For Question (a):

- Make sure you refer to the **text** when making your decisions about the skills you want to include.

- Don't forget to consider any **stage directions** that may be included in the extract.

---

8 (a) There are specific choices in this extract for performers.

 (i) You are going to play Feste.
   Explain **two** ways you would use
   either **physical skills** or **vocal skills**
   to play this character in this extract.

   > In the exam, the question will specify
   > whether you need to cover physical skills **or**
   > vocal skills. **You will not be given a choice.**
   > Make sure you are ready to answer either!

   (4 marks)

 (ii) You are going to play Viola. While disguised as a man, she tells the duke that she is actually in love with him.

   As a performer, give **three** suggestions of how you would use **performance skills** to make it clear to the audience that Viola is hiding the truth throughout this extract.

   You must provide a reason for each suggestion.   **(6 marks)**

 (b) There are specific choices in this extract for a director.

   > For Question (b), you must remember to
   > refer to the **context** in which the text was
   > originally created and performed.

 (i) As a director, discuss how you would use **one** of the **production elements below** to bring this extract to life for your audience.

   You should make reference to the context in which the text was created and performed.

   Choose **one** of the following:

   - costume   • set   • lighting
   - sound   • props/stage furniture   • staging.   **(9 marks)**

In the exam, you will only be given a choice of **three** out of the six production elements listed above for this question. You might get **any combination** of these options – so be prepared!

(ii) The duke is feeling melancholic about Olivia's unrequited love and passes on his experience to Viola.

As a director, discuss how the performer playing the role of the duke might demonstrate this melancholy to the audience in this extract and the complete play.

You must consider:

- voice
- physicality
- stage directions and stage space. **(12 marks)**

(c) There are specific choices in this extract for designers.

Discuss how you would use **one** design element to enhance the production of this extract for an audience.

> For Question (c), try to demonstrate **how** the selected design element would **improve** the performance for an audience.

Choose **one** of the following:

- costume
- lighting
- props/stage furniture
- set
- sound
- staging. **(14 marks)**

> In the exam, you will only be given a choice of **three** out of the six design elements listed above for this question. You might get **any combination** of these options – so be prepared!

(Total for Question 8 = 45 marks)

TOTAL FOR SECTION A = 45 MARKS

SECTION B: LIVE THEATRE EVALUATION
Answer Questions 9(a) and 9(b) on the performance you have seen.

- Read the question carefully to make sure you understand exactly what you are being asked to do.
- Make sure you understand the command word for each question – there will always be one question asking you to **analyse** and one question asking you to **evaluate**.
- Remember, Question 9 will always include **one performance** question and **one design** question. They could appear in any order, so be prepared!

9 (a)

- In the exam, you will **not** have a choice of question for 9(a) like you have below. You will be asked **either** to write about an element of **performance or** an element of **design**. Make sure you are ready to write about either!
- Question 9(a) will ask you to **analyse**. This means you need to select key skills or ideas from the performance you have seen and say **how** the performers or designers explored them.

EITHER

(i) Analyse how levels were used in the staging of the performance to indicate the character relationships for an audience.   **(6 marks)**

OR

(ii) Analyse how body language was used in a key moment of the performance to show relationships between characters.   **(6 marks)**

(b)

- In the exam, you will **not** have a choice of question for 9(b) like you have below. You will be asked **either** to write about an element of **performance or** an element of **design**. Make sure you are ready to write about either!
- Question 9(b) will ask you to **evaluate**. This means you need to form a judgement about whether an idea or performance element has worked or not, giving effective supporting evidence.

EITHER

(i) Evaluate how performance skills were used to create mood at a key moment in the performance.   **(9 marks)**

OR

(ii) Evaluate how volume was used in the performance to create atmosphere for the audience.   **(9 marks)**

(Total for Question 9 = 15 marks)

TOTAL FOR SECTION B = 15 MARKS

TOTAL FOR PAPER = 60 MARKS

SECTION A: BRINGING TEXTS TO LIFE

Indicate which prescribed text you are answering by marking a cross in the box ☒ **. If you change your mind, put a line through the box** ☒ **and then indicate your new question with a cross** ☒ **.**

Chosen performance text:		
1 – *1984* ☒		**5 – *DNA*** ☒
2 – *An Inspector Calls* ☒		**6 – *Dr Korczak's Example*** ☒
3 – *Blue Stockings* ☒		**7 – *Government Inspector*** ☒
4 – *The Crucible* ☒		**8 – *Twelfth Night*** ☒

Question (a)(i)   **(4 marks)**

> The most successful answers to Question (a)(i) will include **reasons**. Justify your reasons and **explain why** you have chosen to use those skills. Make sure you:
> - refer to the skills specified in the question – vocal **or** physical
> - focus on the correct number of skills, as specified in the question
> - use the correct technical vocabulary to support your answer and show your understanding.

Tick which skills you are going write about for this practice question.

(i) Physical ☐

(ii) Vocal ☐

> **Remember**: in the exam, the question will tell you which skills to write about – physical skills **or** vocal skills. **You will not be given a choice.**

....

....

....

....

....

....

....

....

....

....

....

....

....

....

Question (a)(ii)   **(6 marks)**

> The most successful answers to Question (a)(ii) will include **reasons**. Justify your reasons and **explain why** you have chosen to use those skills. Make sure you:
> - refer to the appropriate skills specified in the question – performance skills include **both vocal and physical** skills
> - focus on the correct number of skills, as specified in the question
> - use the correct technical vocabulary to support your answer and show your understanding.

....

....

....

....

....

....

....

....

....

....

....

....

....

....

....

....

....

....

....

....

....

....

....

Question (b)(i)   **(9 marks)**

> The most successful answers to Question (b)(i) will include **reasons**. Justify your reasons and **explain** your ideas. Make sure you:
> - focus only on **one** production element, as specified in the question
> - refer **clearly and explicitly** to the production element you have selected, giving **examples** of how you would use your chosen element to enhance the performance for the audience
> - refer to the **context** in which the text was created and performed
> - use the correct technical vocabulary to support your answer and show your understanding.

Chosen production element:

Costume ☐   **Lighting** ☐   **Props/Stage furniture** ☐

Set ☐   **Sound** ☐   **Staging** ☐

> In the exam, you will not indicate your production element in this way. Instead, you will need to make it very clear in the opening part of your answer which production element you are writing about. Try to do this in this practice question, too.
>
> **Remember**: in the exam, you will only be given **three** production elements to choose from for this question.

....

....

....

....

....

....

....

....

....

....

....

....

....

....

....

....

....

....

....

Had a go ☐ **Nearly there** ☐ **Nailed it!** ☐

Question (b)(ii)   (12 marks)

> The most successful answers to Question (b)(ii) will focus on how a director will work with a performer to communicate specific intentions. Providing **examples** will help you to **justify** your ideas. Make sure you:
> - refer to the elements specified in the question – voice, physicality, stage directions and stage space
> - place the audience at the heart of your response
> - use the correct technical vocabulary to support your answer and show your understanding.

....

....

....

....

....

....

....

....

....

....

....

....

....

....

....

....

....

....

....

....

....

....

....

....

....

Question (c)   **(14 marks)**

The most successful answers to Question (c) will focus on demonstrating how the selected design element could be used to enhance the production of the extract. Providing **examples** will help you to **justify** your decisions. Make sure you:

- refer to the use of the element and demonstrate understanding of how the selected element may support performance decisions (such as character status or reflecting the style/genre)
- provide reasons for all decisions made
- use the correct technical vocabulary to support your answer and show your understanding.

Chosen design element:

Costume ☐   **Lighting** ☐   **Props/Stage furniture** ☐

Set ☐   **Sound** ☐   **Staging** ☐

In the exam, you will not indicate your design element in this way. Instead, you will need to make it very clear in the opening part of your answer which design element you are writing about. Try to do this in this practice question, too.

Remember: in the exam, you will only be given **three** design elements to choose from for this question.

....

....

....

....

....

....

....

....

....

....

....

....

....

....

....

....

....

....

....

....

....

....

....

....

....

....

....

....

....

....

....

....

....

....

....

....

....

....

....

....

....

....

....

....

....

....

....

....

....

....

....

....

TOTAL FOR SECTION A = 45 MARKS

SECTION B: LIVE THEATRE EVALUATION

Answer both questions in this section on the performance you have seen.

Write the title, venue and date of the performance you have seen in the space below.

Performance details

Title:...

Venue:...

Date seen:...

Question 9(a)   **(6 marks)**

> The most successful answers for Question 9(a) will **analyse** the live performance to demonstrate a clear understanding of the production. Make sure you:
> - focus on the part of the performance specified in the question (such as 'beginning', 'end' or 'key moment'); alternatively, the question could refer to the whole performance
> - analyse the key element required as well as the impact that element had on the audience.

Tick which element you are going write about for this practice question:

(i) Design   ☐   **Remember**: in the exam, the question will tell
                                          you which element to write about – performance
(ii) Performance   ☐   **or** design. **You will not be given a choice.**

....

....

....

....

....

....

....

....

....

....

....

....

....

....
....
....
....
....
....
....
....
....
....
....
....
....
....
....
....
....
....
....
....
....
....
....
....
....
....
....
....
....
....

Question 9(b)   **(9 marks)**

Question 9(b) will always ask you to **evaluate**. You need to make sure you:
- demonstrate a clear understanding of the techniques used
- use your understanding to draw a **conclusion** about how successful (or not) the selected techniques were.

Tick which element you are going write about for this practice question:

(i) Design   ☐

(ii) Performance   ☐

> **Remember**: in the exam, the question will tell you which element to write about – performance or design. **You will not be given a choice.**

....

....

....

....

....

....

....

....

....

....

....

....

....

....

....

....

....

....

....

....

....

....

....

....

....

....

....

....

....

....

....

....

....

....

....

....

....

....

....

....

....

....

....

....

....

....

....

....

TOTAL FOR SECTION B = 15 MARKS

TOTAL FOR PAPER = 60 MARKS

Answers

Where an exemplar answer is given, this is not necessarily the only correct response. In most cases there is a range of responses that can gain full marks. Example answers may be based on one of the eight possible performance texts for Edexcel GCSE Drama.

THEATRE MAKERS
1. Key roles in the theatre
1 (a) *Performer:*
   - uses physical and vocal skills with control
   - interprets and develops characterisation
   - conveys the story/narrative to an audience.

   (b) *Designer:*
   - designs the different production elements required for the performance (such as lighting, sound, costume)
   - works with the director to create a consistent approach to the production
   - provides creative solutions to any design-related problems that may occur.

   (c) *Director:*
   - has overall creative control over the entire production
   - decides on the overall style of production
   - works alongside designers to create a consistent approach to the production.

2 (a) performer; (b) designer; (c) director; (d) director; (e) performer; (f) designer

2. The audience
1 The audience should be placed at the <u>centre</u> of every decision made relating to a performance. It is the responsibility of the entire <u>production team</u> to ensure the play successfully communicates key <u>themes</u> and the agreed purpose to an audience. Decisions such as where a performer is positioned on stage, or the way a line is delivered, can have a powerful impact on an <u>audience</u>, controlling their reaction. Each role within the production will consider different things. A <u>performer</u> may ask how they want the audience to feel about the character they are portraying. A <u>designer</u> may ask how they want the audience to react to the choices made relating to lighting, costume, sound or set. A <u>director</u> will consider where the audience may be positioned and what impact this will have on their <u>perspective</u> of the events on stage.

2 (a) *Content and material*: The themes, story or characters may be aimed at a particular group of people who have something in common and therefore have a similar interest. This may include almost anything, such as a shared location, history, gender, religion or even a hobby.

   (b) *Language*: This may include the actual language spoken in the performance (for example, English, Urdu, Polish). It may also refer to the type of words used in a performance. For example, swearing or using modern slang words may be more appropriate for a younger target audience, whereas older audiences may find the words offensive.

   (c) *Themes and issues*: These may be of specific interest to a specific target audience. For example, *Blue Stockings* is a play about the fight to allow women to graduate, so the target audience may be those interested in gender equality. *DNA* is a play about teenagers involved in covering up a crime, so the target audience may be teenagers and young adults.

3 The target audience for this performance is communities and younger people. The idea that the monologues are linked by flashbacks will try to demonstrate that this old man was once like the people watching the performance and that it is possible that they may also be heading the same way. It will encourage people within the community to think about older individuals living nearby who may be lonely, and may influence them to reach out to or communicate more with them.

3. Theatrical concepts
1 (a) genre; (b) proxemics; (c) stage directions; (d) form; (e) style; (f) structure; (g) staging; (h) context

2 *Social, historical and cultural contexts*:
   (a) Definition: When, or under what circumstances, a play was written.
   (b) Impact on performance: Helps to put the play in perspective and gives directors, designers and performers the context for the production. It can provide important clues about what the play is about, and the themes and issues contained within the play.

   Stage directions:
   (a) Definition: The playwright's instructions about what performers should do, and how, and as well as how the play should look and sound.
   (b) Impact on performance: Gives clues as to how the playwright visualised the play, and helps with elements such as set, lighting, sound effects, props, costume, staging and proxemics, as well as how a character may say a line or move on stage.

   Genre:
   (a) Definition: The category or the type of play.
   (b) Impact on performance: Understanding the genre can help theatre makers reach important decisions about the style and atmosphere of a production.

   Staging:
   (a) Definition: The physical space in which the production is performed.
   (b) Impact on performance: Effective use of staging can have a huge impact on the perspective of the audience. It may bring the action into the audience and make the performance more interactive. Additionally, it may help to communicate important information, such as relationships and status, through the use of levels.

4. Conventions and terminology
1 *Directly addressing the audience*: This is a powerful way for a character to express important information about the situation. It may convey the character's inner thoughts or place a situation in context. Directly addressing the audience is often a signal that other characters on stage cannot hear what is being said.

   Symbolism in costume and set: Representing ideas, themes and issues symbolically through costume and set can provide vital clues as to the type of character the audience are seeing. It can also act as a reminder of the important themes and issues at the heart of the play.

   Use of multimedia (such as music and projection): As well as being able to indicate important information such as location and era, multimedia can also have a huge impact on the mood and atmosphere of a performance.

Use of multi-role (where a performer plays more than one character): This is an effective way to include a wider range of characters without using a larger cast of performers. Multi-role can also be an effective tool to reinforce a more abstract style of theatre, as the audience will see the same performer portraying different roles.

2   *To prove my knowledge and understanding of theatre-making*: Using the correct terminology indicates that I have grasped different ideas and concepts. Also, that I have a clear understanding about the things I am talking about, whether these are ideas relating to the actual performance or the themes of the play.

3   *To communicate my ideas and intentions clearly, and to avoid confusion*: By using the correct theatre terminology, I will be more able to clearly express what it is I am trying to say. Using the correct terminology will help to indicate exactly which theatre-making role I am referring to, and to then convey my ideas and thoughts with clarity.

4   *To show my understanding of the different roles in theatre-making*: The exam requires me to answer questions from three different perspectives – performer, director and designer. By using the correct terminology, I will be able to demonstrate that I understand the difference between each of these roles, as well as how they combine to produce a performance.

5   *To ensure my answers are strong*: As there is limited time in the exam, I need to ensure that all the answers I give are clear and efficient, and that it is easy to understand exactly what I am trying to say. I also need to ensure that I have enough time to answer all of the questions in the 90 minutes allowed for the exam. Using the correct terminology will help me to express my ideas efficiently.

Performer
5. The performer

1   A performer uses a range of skills to communicate with an audience, including vocal skills, physical skills, characterisation and use of space. During rehearsals, performers will often work with directors and designers to create a successful performance. A performer will also usually work as part of an ensemble, being an effective member of a team. They will need to develop their own interpretation of a character, as well as exploring the text in as much depth as possible. However, the most important thing for a performer to consider is the relationship they develop with the audience.

2   *Primary responsibility of the performer*: communicating character; engaging with the audience; applying the overall vision in performance.
    Primary responsibility of the director: creating an overall vision for the performance.

3   One way I would play the role of Karen would be to stare wide-eyed and open-mouthed as Elizabeth walked away, my eyes following her. I would then slowly turn my head towards the box, making it the focus of attention. Then, after a slight pause to show I was deep in thought about what to do next, I would quickly move to the door, located stage right, and turn my head upstage and then directly into the wings, as if I were looking to see if anyone were there. Then I would almost run back to the box and, taking advantage of all of the time I have, grab it, trying to

conceal it under my clothing, run back to the doorway, look again, repeating the actions from just before and quickly run out.

6. Tone and intonation

1   **(a)** emotions; **(b)** relationships; **(c)** intentions; **(d)** subtext.

2   **(a)** Tone is the way in which a performer gets across the meaning of what a character is saying. For example, if a character feels angry, the performer may use a very bitter tone to their voice, perhaps spitting out the words and making the end of each word very clipped.

    (b) Intonation is the way the performer's voice rises and falls to provide more interest and variation for the audience. This will help to make the speech patterns more natural, as well as helping to convey the meaning a performer is trying to communicate to the audience. For example, to support the anger of the character from the above answer for 2(a), a performer could include a rising intonation to a specific word, so helping to emphasise that word and provide a deeper and clearer meaning.

3   **(a)** *Concern/worry*: To show that Robert is genuinely concerned, I would emphasise the words 'Finally', 'made' and 'worried' with a sincere and relieved tone. I would also raise the intonation for these words to communicate this emphasis to the audience.

    (b) *Anger*: Here, to show that Robert is angry that he has been made to wait, I would use a short, clipped tone to the word 'Finally', with a falling intonation. Then I would say the words 'so', 'earth' and 'sick' with a deeply sarcastic tone to show that I have not been worried about the person themselves, but that I have other concerns that have made me angry.

4   **(a)** *Hopelessness*: To show that Geeta views the situation as hopeless, my voice would be quite monotone to indicate that I am feeling depressed. Each sentence would be spoken slowly and end with a slightly falling intonation to make it appear as though I feel overwhelmed by my situation and powerless to change it.

    (b) *Enthusiasm*: I would speak with a clipped, short tone that would allow me to move through the lines with some speed. My tone would be positive and upbeat. I would speak with a raised intonation at the end of sentences to indicate a great energy and excitement in my voice. This would be particularly noticeable for the final question, where I would raise the final syllable of 'heavy' to show my interest in the object in the bag.

7. Pause and pitch

1   **(a)** Their age – for example, very young, young, very old.
    (b) Their background – for example, culture, language, where they grew up.
    (c) Their emotional state – how they are feeling at any given moment.
    (d) Their status – how much power they have over others, or that others have over them.

2   **(a)** For example, this could be:
    • ERIN: I'm / not sure what to say, or:
    • ERIN: I'm not / sure what to say, or:
    • ERIN: I'm not sure / what to say, or:
    • ERIN: I'm not sure what / to say…
    Any choice is fine provided the decision is justified in part (b).

    (b) This shows that Erin is trying to think of what to say, and the pause actually reflects the fact that she really does not know what to say.

3 *Context*: Erin has manipulated Rose into stealing a mobile phone. Rose has been caught and is being taken away. Erin pretends to be surprised, while Rose begins to panic.

Explanation: In the first line, Erin speaks with a low tone at an even pace. There are no pauses, with a rising tone on the word 'say', emphasising her surprise. Rose speaks with a high pitch, representing her fear at being caught and what is about to happen to her. She pauses between the two sentences, allowing time for her to be taken away. Her second sentence is pitched even higher, showing a rise in tension and desperation, and with a strong emphasis on 'supposed'. Finally, Erin responds after a lengthy pause. Again, this is to indicate the control she has over the situation. This pause will also significantly help to build the tension further.

8. Clarity and pace

1 (a) The judge must have the highest status in the courtroom. Therefore, the clarity of the words must be able to represent this high status. Each word is spoken deliberately and clearly, emphasising the end of each word with precision. A very short pause before 'guilty' would allow a slight emphasis on the 'g' and this emphasis would then also aid the clarity of the words. This clarity will also indicate that the decision has been a considered one and has not been rushed. Additionally, the delivery of the sentence is very serious and, therefore, the clarity of the speech would reflect the formality of the occasion.

(b) To make the repeated words effective and have meaning, there should be a variation in the way each word is delivered. This is also important as they are the last words Mary says as she is removed from the court. The first 'Please!' should be short and clipped, as if making the request as quickly as she can. Then the second 'Please!' would be longer, with the final 'Please!' very long and trailing into a longer sob as Mary desperately tries to change the judge's mind.

(c) Mary must be overcome with emotion and indicate to the audience that she is absolutely terrified. The stage directions make it clear that she is vocalising her emotions throughout the judge's speech. Her sobbing would contain mumbled words, such as 'no' and 'please', foreshadowing the words she uses in her line at the end of the extract. This mumbling would be deliberately less clear than the other spoken dialogue as this communicates the overwhelming emotions Mary is feeling. This mumbling would build up in pace until she hears the actual sentence passed, where she would then shriek the word 'No!'. At this point, the pace would rapidly increase and words would be spoken with greater clarity to show her desperation and fear of being taken away from her family, as well as trying to get her final say as she is removed from the court.

9. Accent and inflection

1 (a) character status; **(b)** social class of the character; **(c)** the city, region or country the character is from; **(d)** where the play is set.

2 I would use the native accents for each of the different groups. For example, Scottish for the Scots rebels and Welsh accents for the Merthyr Tydfil rebels. This use of accents would help the audience fully appreciate exactly where the characters have come from and demonstrate

that those who were transported were from a very broad geographical and cultural range.

3 (a) To make this line into a question, I would use a rising inflection at the end of the sentence, specifically on the word 'idea'.

(b) To make this line into a statement, I would use a falling inflection on the words 'actually thought' and 'idea'.

10. Emphasis and volume

1 (a) '*I think there is a solution*': This means that Andrew himself believes that there is a solution to the problem.

(b) '*I think there is a solution*': This indicates that Andrew thinks there might be a possible solution, but he is not completely sure.

(c) '*I think there is a solution*': This suggests that Andrew has already expressed an opinion that there is a solution, but is not being listened to.

2 (a) If the line were shouted it could show that: Marie is angry with Andrew and frustrated that he does not understand that she used to trust the other person.

(b) If the line were whispered it could show that: Marie is feeling betrayed by the other person and is trying hard to undersand how they could have let her down so badly.

3 *Volume*: quiet, booming, diminuendo, whispering, softly, crescendo
Tone: monotone, nasally

11. Diction and nuance

1 (a) *Context 1*: Kelly is terrified of Ali and Breanna: If I were playing Kelly, I would speak the first line with a slight stutter on the word 'I'm' to show fear. I would then speak the second line with pace and energy to show I was trying to get all of my explanation out before being interrupted. I would then give a slight pause before saying, quite definitely, 'But I didn't take it with me'.

(b) *Context 2*: Breanna and Kelly are working together: I would say Breanna's opening line quite deliberately and with a steady pace, as if I were showing Kelly that I was following the agreed story. Kelly could reinforce this by copying the pattern of speech and emphasising the last words to show the audience that Kelly is almost prompting Breanna to give the correct, agreed answer.

2 (a) articulation; **(b)** pronunciation; **(c)** inflection; **(d)** hint; **(e)** shading; **(f)** trace; **(g)** enunciation; **(h)** suggestion

3 *Diction*: enunciation, pronunciation, inflection, articulation
Nuance: shading, suggestion, trace, hint

12. Facial expression and body language

1 Emotions conveyed through facial expression: fear, sadness, happiness, anger, contempt, disgust, surprise.

2 The 'crash' sound effect indicates that this is a sudden event that gives Shaheera a shock, scaring her. Therefore, she would turn her body suddenly, allowing her head to rotate further than her body, as if she were trying to protect her vital organs. As she turns, her arms would rise to protect her face, again enabling her body language to show that she is reacting mainly on instinct and in an instant. This could be further backed up by Shaheera ducking down in an attempt to make her body smaller and therefore less likely to be hit by any objects that may be flung into the room.

The emotion changes suddenly when Shaheera realises the person making the noise is friendly. Therefore, the body language will change from a tense and rigid state to one of relief. Shaheera will return to her full height and her shoulders will drop as the tension leaves her body, to show the audience that she realises that the situation is no longer threatening.

3   This example answer is based on *An Inspector Calls*; the chosen character is Sheila; the moment described is when Sheila enters the dining room and hears about Eva's death for the first time:

As Sheila enters the dining room, she is relaxed and very happy. She has just become engaged and the stage direction says she speaks her line 'gaily'. Her facial expression is joyous, with a large smile, and she almost skips into the room, giving an impression of both youth and carefree innocence. A low level of shock replaces this when she hears about how Eva died. When she speaks the line 'Oh – how horrible…', her body language includes clenched hands, gripped together in front of her chest in an almost prayer-like gesture to show her distress. Sheila would stand upright, to reflect her upbringing and social status. Additionally, her facial expression would change to that of slight shock and she would be unable to keep eye contact with the Inspector. This would show Sheila's distress and also the uncomfortable emotions he stirs in the other characters, as she cannot face him directly. This reflects the relationship Sheila develops with the Inspector, in which he takes control over her and is able to raise his status above hers.

13. Gesture and proxemics

1   (a) *High status*: Place the highest status character upstage, looking downstage and separate to the other characters on stage.
    (b) *Love*: Place the two lovers close together on stage, facing each other and able to make physical contact.
    (c) *Hate*: Place the characters a long way apart from each other on stage. Using the space, have at least one character with their back turned to the other, if required.
    (d) *Fear*: Place the character(s) who are fearful away from the source of fear, but give them a line of sight to indicate to the audience exactly what the cause of the fear is.

2   (a) The central character stands upstage, raised above the others. He points with a strong, outstretched arm directly at the door to indicate they must leave.
    (b) The character should be close to the torturer, on their knees and making a begging gesture, holding both hands together and raised above the head.
    (c) As she gives up the chase, the character stands in the middle of the stage, turns directly to the audience and clicks her fingers as she swings her arm across her body.
    (d) As the plan is being hatched, the group members, all huddled closely together to indicate they are discussing something secret, would rub their hands together in glee.

14. Stance and stillness

1   (a) status; (b) age; (c) gender; (d) emotional state; (e) profession; (f) physical well-being
2   (c) Posture
3   For example:
    (a) *Scenario 1*: A character may be gripped by a terrifying fear that almost physically paralyses them and prevents them from running away. For example, being caught by a gunman as they are trying to sneak out to safety without being seen.

    (b) *Scenario 2*: A character might be comically caught doing something they should not be doing and the performer could use sudden stillness to show being caught in the act. For example, the performer could be caught eating someone else's sandwich and freeze at the moment they are about to take a huge bite.

4   This example answer uses *Twelfth Night* as the performance text:
    (a) *Moment 1*: When Sir Andrew first meets Maria (Act 1, Scene 3) and mistakenly thinks she is called Mistress Accost, Maria might stand still, looking to the audience to pause the action for a moment, to reinforce that she thinks he is ridiculous.
    (b) *Moment 2*: When two officers enter to arrest Antonio (Act 3, Scene 4), Antonio might suddenly stand still, demonstrating a moment of realisation that he is in serious trouble and about to be taken away in a city where he is a man wanted for serious crimes.

15. Movement and spatial awareness

1   Words to describe movement: stagger, tumble, march, amble, creep, scramble, burst, dash, trot, edge, plod, glide
2   He/She:
    • tumbled/downstage/from a combination of being pushed and falling down the slope
    • skated/from upstage left/joyfully and full of love
    • crept/across centre stage/fearfully hiding from the burglar
    • strode briskly/to upstage right/determined to give the child a serious telling off.

3   To show that my character is frightened using spatial awareness, I might push myself up into a tight space, physically backing myself into a corner. This would show an audience that my character is looking for some sort of protection and wants to hide away.

16. Personality and purpose

1   *Positive personality traits*: philosophical, sincere, witty, compassionate, versatile, amiable, understanding, modest
    Negative personality traits: interfering, obstinate, indiscrete, truculent, vengeful, pompous, aloof, self-centred
2   This example answer uses *1984* as the performance text:
    (a) *Character*: Winston; *Personality traits*: brave, foolish, desperate; *Purpose in play*: central character – through him, the audience are shown what the Party is capable of.
    (b) *Character*: O'Brien; *Personality traits*: cruel, deceitful, controlling; *Purpose in play*: embodiment of the Party; indicates what they are willing to do to maintain control.
    (c) *Character*: Julia; *Personality traits*: passionate, confident, powerful; *Purpose in play*: she is the opposite of the Party – emotional and a catalyst for Winston to break free.
3   This example answer uses *1984* as the performance text and the personality traits for Winston identified in Question 2:
    • Winston shows bravery when he stands up to O'Brien during the torture scene. He knows that more pain is coming – and that he cannot hold out forever – but he is determined not to betray Julia.
    • Winston is foolish when he agrees to continue seeing Julia. He knows that this will lead to their arrests, but he continues the relationship anyway.

- Winston is desperate when he is taken to Room 101. When faced with his greatest fear – the rats – he finally betrays Julia and begs that they do it to her rather than him.

17. Motives, aims and objectives

1 (a) *Aims and objectives*: What the character wants or needs to achieve in either a scene or over the whole play.
   (b) *Motive*: The reasons or purpose a character has for doing what they do in order to achieve their aims and objectives.

2 (a) The man is in love with her and is trying to win the woman's affections.
   (b) The politician is concerned that his own corruption will be exposed and is trying to hide all evidence from the visitor.
   (c) The orphan is starving, having not eaten properly for many weeks. He/she is desperate.

3 This example answer is based on *An Inspector Calls*.
   Character name: Mr Birling
   Aims/objectives with examples:
   (a) Birling's aim is to protect his reputation, business and wealth (shown by his arguments with the Inspector).
   (b) Birling wants to demonstrate his high status to the Inspector (he mentions he is a magistrate and that he is friends with the Chief Constable).
   (c) Birling wants to undermine the Inspector to his family (he telephones the Chief Constable to check if Inspector Goole is a genuine police officer).
   Character name: Sheila
   Aims/objectives with examples:
   (a) She wants to be seen as a grown adult (she begins to empathise with Eva Smith).
   (b) She tries to stop her mother from making the same mistakes under questioning from the Inspector (she begs her mother to stop arguing back and to listen to her).
   (c) Sheila wants her parents to realise they have responsibilities as well as privileges (she insists that, even though Goole is not a real police officer, it is the facts relating to Eva Smith that really matter).

18. Development and relationships

1 Character development refers to the way in which a character evolves and changes from the beginning to the end of the play.

2 This example answer is based on *Blue Stockings*.
   Tess:
   - *Beginning*: She is a determined, hard-working and independent young woman who plans to further her education as much as she can.
   - *Middle*: Her feelings for Ralph mean that she is becoming blinded by love. This is distracting her from her studies and she is beginning to feel the pressure. In turn, this leads to strain within her relationships with others.
   - *End*: Reeling from the shock of failing her course, she is on the brink of giving up. However, at the last moment, her resilience returns and she is even more determined than before.
   Will:
   - *Beginning*: A serious individual who initially pretends he does not know Tess. He struggles to fit in with the other men.
   - *Middle*: He struggles to keep his feelings for Tess to himself and, becoming overprotective of her, he struggles even more to fit in with the other men.

- *End*: He is supportive of the campaign to allow women to graduate. Will is also very encouraging towards Tess, persuading her to return to Girton.
Holmes:
- *Beginning*: A rowdy young man, he is very much a part of the group of young men who see the women as something of a novelty.
- *Middle*: His views towards women become even more fixed and he expresses those views increasingly vocally.
- *End*: Although he protests against graduation for women, he recognises the struggle the women have experienced and, despite the fact he still disagrees with them, declares his deep respect for their fight.

3 This example answer is based on the character of Holmes in *Blue Stockings*.
   (a) A key relationship for Holmes is his relationship with Lloyd.
   (b) Rowdy, pressured, immature.
   (c) Holmes feels that he has to fit in and is happy to follow Lloyd's lead. However, as Lloyd becomes increasingly extreme in his views and actions relating to the young women, Holmes eventually takes more of a stand, expressing his respect (although not his agreement) for the women's cause.

19. Research and impact

1 (a) Suggested aspects: time period, character backstory, social/political events, location(s) of the play, relationships and effects on others, character types, jobs and roles, themes and issues.
   (b) Your developed concept maps should be based on your performance text. The example answer below is based on *The Crucible*.
   - *Time period*: 1692
   - *Location(s) of the play*: Salem, Massachusetts
   - *Social/political events*: The power of the Church and lack of security relating to the colonisation of America. Can also be linked to McCarthy trials in the 1940s and 1950s.
   - *Character types*: High-status religious leaders, rich landowners, vulnerable villagers
   - *Relationships and effects on others*: The love triangle between Proctor, Elizabeth and Abigail has a devastating impact on the rest of the village.
   - *Character backstory*: Abigail Williams (a servant girl) has an affair with John Proctor, leading to her being dismissed by Elizabeth Proctor (John's wife). Abigail is deeply in love with John and wants to win him back, leading to her trying to summon the devil and make a potion to kill Elizabeth.
   - *Jobs and roles*: Church leaders, the Deputy Governor of the Province, rich landowners, poor tenant farmers
   - *Themes and issues*: The power of the state over the individual; betrayal; the collapse of trust in the community

2 This example answer is based on *1984*.
   (a) *Character name*: Julia
   Impact when first enters stage: Julia first enters the stage as 'The Waitress', and Winston is terrified of her. She should also have this impact on the audience. Therefore, Julia should come across as very formal, following the requirements of the Party, and with a piercing stare.

(b) *Character name*: Charrington

Charrington should appear as a friendly character who is both approachable and safe. The audience should feel that Charrington is similar to Winston in his feelings about the Party and that, because of this opinion, Winston is able to relax somewhat and lower his guard around him.

20. Still images and asides

1 voice, mime

2 **(a)** By facing the audience and directly addressing them when speaking.

(b) By moving downstage towards the audience, to distance themselves from the rest of the action.

(c) By raising their hand to their mouth and using a stage whisper, to show they do not want the other characters on stage to hear what is being said.

3 This example answer is based on *Twelfth Night*:

When Antonio is arrested in *Twelfth Night*, Act 3, Scene 4, he is shocked how Viola (who he thinks is Sebastian) treats him. This leads Antonio to a degree of desperation followed by complete resignation. When performing Antonio, I would show this resignation in a still image: I would slump my shoulders and allow my arms to droop down by my sides. My head would also fall forwards and my facial expression would have a heavily knitted brow. I would wear a frown to show how disappointed I was that the man (I thought) I had saved was now rejecting my call for help. Viola would be standing upstage, slightly distancing herself from Antonio, to show her confusion – although her offer to lend Antonio money does show some gratitude. Antonio would be flanked by the two officers who are ready to take him away, standing tall and straight to indicate their status. Sir Toby, Sir Andrew and Fabian all stand to the side, fearful and confused by the events; this is shown by them cowering yet watching events unfold with curiosity.

21. Monologue and physical theatre

1 **(a)** Include physicality and movement – consider what the character is doing.

(b) Ensure there is vocal variety and that the voice reflects the character's emotions.

(c) Be clear about who the monologue is aimed at (for example, the audience or other characters on stage).

2 Physical theatre is an abstract theatrical style in which performers use their bodies to create and represent a range of ideas and objects to an audience. Physical theatre is often very collaborative, visually exciting and includes a high degree of movement. Performers rely on each other for support and security on stage – for example, when a performer is being lifted or held in the air by the other cast members.

3 **(a)** *An arrest*: An arresting officer moves towards the person being arrested. The performers engage in a sequence where the officer tries to grab the accused, who then maintains contact with the officer's body but slides around the officer's arms and legs to represent resisting arrest.

(b) *A disagreement*: An arguing group of friends represent the verbal disagreement through a series of physical theatre lifts. Whoever is winning the argument is raised up by the rest of the group to reflect the higher status they have at that point. When they are losing the argument, the group will then bring them lower to the ground.

(c) *Love*: To show they are in love, a couple stand facing each other and slowly begin to move in a synchronised way. Simple mirroring gestures with the hands steadily evolve into full, supportive lifts. This indicates they are acting as one couple supporting each other, as opposed to two separate individuals.

(d) *Vandalism*: Two people stand facing an imaginary wall (facing the audience). One uses exaggerated movements to mime spraying paint. The other performer then repeats the same sequence. As confidence grows, the sequences between the two performers gather pace until they are both synchronised at a fast speed.

22. Narration and multi-role

1 **(a)** voice; **(b)** accent; **(c)** gesture; **(d)** facial expression; **(e)** costume; **(f)** hair; **(g)** personal props; **(h)** movement

2 Example answer:

If I were playing Kofi, I would start by standing upstage centre, initially hidden by the smoke from the explosion. From there, I would speak my first line, but I would remain unseen by the audience. Using a long pause, I would then move downstage so that the audience can see me as well as hear me for my second line. Katie would also be visible, collapsed on the ground and I would move towards her, shifting my attention and focus from the audience to her and then back again to show that I was a link between the audience and the action on stage. I would then move closer to Katie, although I would not actually interact with her or make any contact. However, I would use gesture to reflect her actions, and she would be using mime, physically mirroring my words. The tone of my voice, indicating the urgency and the fear that Katie is feeling, would communicate the emotional intensity of the scene to the audience. As the speech ends, I would drift to stage right, leaving Katie as the central focus and using a vocal tone to finish the line as a cliffhanger before allowing the action to continue.

23. Mime, flashback and flash forward

1 **(a)** True; **(b)** False; **(c)** True; **(d)** True

2 A mimed sequence can be a very effective way to represent a range of things that would not work so effectively if done naturalistically, such as moving between time frames or portraying a dramatic event such as a riot or a fight, or two characters falling in love.

3 This example answer is based on *Dr Korczak's Example*:

At the beginning of the performance, the 'Actor' is explaining the context of the story (such as the location and time period – the Jewish ghetto in Nazi-occupied Warsaw, summer 1942). As this is happening, the performer playing the role of Adzio could be silently portraying the key life events that led to him stealing an apple from the market stall. These events would include how Adzio lost his parents and was then forced to fend for himself on the streets. The flashbacks would be seen as a series of still images linked with a short mime sequence between each one; this would help to place both the image and also the actions in context. This would then help the audience to understand why Adzio behaves as he does at the start of the play.

24. Symbolism and split scene

1 **(a)** *Love*: A performer could symbolise love through gesture, such as raising a hand to their chest and laying the hand over their heart.

(b) *Hate*: A performer could use a gesture of clenched teeth or jaw and a facial expression of anger. Additionally, they could pretend to spit on the ground towards the object of their hate.

(c) *Disgust*: A performer could screw up their face and use body language to show slight physical convulsions, as though they might be about to vomit.

(d) *Wealth*: A character could use exaggerated gesture to highlight their possessions, such as expensive jewellery or a valuable item such as a high-end mobile phone.

2 (a) If I were playing Amar, I would focus on the action with Jimmi. It would be important to indicate to the audience that this action takes place in a totally different location to where Jenni and Dawn are, so I would not look at the girls at all. When the girls are speaking, I would completely freeze, to ensure the audience knows I am not part of the girls' scene.

(b) I would ensure that I remained totally still during the opening scene with the boys. This would tell the audience that I am not in any way a part of that scene and I could not hear them. I would put all of my attention on what Dawn is saying and ensure I am facing her completely. I would also emphasise to the audience my disgust about the use of leather, as this would be an immediate reflection of what Amar has just said.

25. Caricature and choral speaking

1 (a) clarity; (b) synchronised speech; (c) projection; (d) tone; (e) volume

2 Caricature is an <u>exaggeration</u> of a character's features. As a performer, therefore, you need to consider which aspects of a <u>character</u> you want to exaggerate, to give the <u>audience</u> a clearer understanding of the character's <u>function</u> in the play. For example, you may have a character with a lot of <u>nervous</u> energy or who is afraid, and you could highlight this through exaggerated use of <u>movement</u> or over-the-top reactions.

3 This example answer is based on *Government Inspector*:

(a) *Character 1*: The Mayor
The Mayor is a highly energetic character who is terrified of being arrested for corruption when he hears a Government Inspector is coming. To show this nervous energy, I would move in very short, fast bursts of energy, never staying in one place for any period of time. Coupled to this, I would use huge gestures, often waving my arms in a seemingly uncontrolled manner. When threatening or accusing people of not doing their jobs, I would then point, using almost my whole arm. This would show how on edge I am.

(b) *Character 2*: Khlestakov
When Khlestakov dines at the Mayor's house, he is entertaining people with his stories. These are exaggerated and so to reflect this his facial expressions, gestures will also be exaggerated, creating a caricature. I would reflect parts of the story, such as his claim regarding important guests waiting to speak with him and pacing in his hallway, by taking large strides across the stage, moving from character to character.

Director
26. The director

1 A director has overall <u>creative control</u> of the performance. During rehearsals, directors will often have to work with <u>performers</u> and <u>designers</u> in order to create a successful performance. The director also needs to lead the <u>team</u> and be an effective team member at the same time. A director will develop a creative vision for the play and be clear about the <u>style</u> and <u>genre</u> they want to use in the production. One of the most important things for a director to consider is the key points of the play they wish to convey and how they can <u>communicate</u> these to an audience.

2 *Primary responsibility of the director*: creating an overall vision for the performance; organising and running rehearsals; providing the performers with detailed feedback to aid improvements.
Primary responsibility of the designer: producing final costume designs.

3 This example answer uses lighting as the chosen production element:
As the stage direction requires Karen to be 'fearful', I would want the audience to experience the tension she is feeling. The source of that tension must come from the box and from what is inside it. Therefore, I would want the stage lit with a low light, using a range of blue and green washes, to give the space an eerie feeling. In order to highlight the key areas of the stage, I would ask for a soft-edged spotlight to indicate the location of the door, placed upstage left. I would also ask for a narrow beam, hard-edged spotlight to illuminate the box on the floor, emphasising the source of the tension.

27. Messages and subtext

1 This example answer is based on *Blue Stockings*:
(a) Equal opportunities for women (women demand the right to graduate).
(b) Standing up for principles (Mr Banks is willing to teach the young women despite the risk to his career).
(c) The need to balance our personal and professional lives (Tess neglects her studies because of her relationship with Ralph).
(d) Never giving up (despite failing her course, Tess decides to return the following academic year).

2 Subtext is when a character says or does one thing but actually means something different. For example, a young man retrieves a sentimental item that has been stolen from a young woman; when he returns the item, she says how pleased she is to see the object again – but actually she means she is pleased to see the young man again.

3 (a) 'I'm glad we can put this bag back before I get into trouble.'
(b) 'This present should impress her and help me get my promotion.'
(c) 'Thank goodness the medicine is here. This could save his life.'
(d) 'I am so angry David has messed this up for me. Because he was late, I am the one to suffer.'

28. Genre and style

1 *Genre*: political satire, romantic comedy, social thriller, black comedy, historical drama, mystery
Style: epic theatre, expressionism, physical theatre, naturalism

2 (a) Genre of performance text:
- *1984*: Political satire
- *Blue Stockings*: Historical drama
- *The Crucible*: Historical drama
- *DNA*: Black comedy
- *Dr Korczak's Example*: Historical drama
- *Government Inspector*: Black comedy
- *An Inspector Calls*: Social thriller/mystery
- *Twelfth Night*: Romantic comedy

(b) This example answer (giving a feature of the genre with example) is based on *Twelfth Night*:

- Several different characters falling in love with each other at the same time. For example, Orsino loves Olivia and Olivia loves Cesario (not knowing Cesario's true identity).
- Comedy flows from confusion. For example, Viola, dressed as a man, appears to look the same as her twin brother. When he later arrives in Illyria, the other characters mistake him for Olivia, whereas the audience have a clear perspective of what is happening and can see the cause of the confusion or humour.
- There is a happy ending. For example, the twins are reunited, Viola's identity is revealed, Orsino marries Viola, Olivia marries Sebastian, Sir Toby has married Maria and peace will (hopefully) be made with Malvolio.

29. Types of staging

1 Traverse stage – The audience are on two sides of the performance space.
Theatre-in-the-round – The audience surround the performance space.
Promenade theatre – The audience move around the performance space.
Proscenium arch – The audience are only on one side of the performance space.
Thrust stage – The audience are on three sides of the performance space.

2 **(a)** *Thrust stage*:
Stage plan:

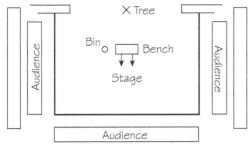

Reasons for chosen plan: I would place the tree at the top of the stage so as not to block the sightlines for the audience. The bench would be upstage, but closer to centre stage than the tree, to give depth on stage. The bench would face downstage to ensure the audience could see the performers clearly. The bin would be next to it, but be quite small to support the sightlines.

(b) *Traverse stage*:
Stage plan:

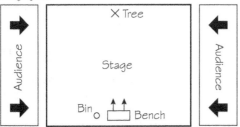

Reasons for chosen plan: I would place the tree at the top of the stage to keep the audience sightlines clear. I would put the bench and bin at the opposite end of the stage, again for sightlines. They would be facing the tree, to give a focal point and to ensure the performers are facing the audience.

30. Consistency and communication

1 This example answer is based on *Twelfth Night*:
   (a) **(i)** *Twelfth Night*; **(ii)** 17th century; **(iii)** proscenium arch
   (b) **(i)** The costumes would be traditional Elizabethan or Shakespearean costumes, reflecting the fashions of the time, including using colours to reflect the status of each character.
   (ii) The set would be relatively simple, remaining empty for much of the time. However, specific locations would be represented by pieces of furniture, such as an ornate chair for Orsino's palace.
   (iii) To reflect the traditions of the time, I would use an all-male cast. This would also enhance the humour of the play.
2 **(a)** *Scenario 1*: Working with the lighting designer, I would flood the stage with a pale blue light, giving the impression of moonlight.
   (b) *Scenario 2*: I would ask the performer playing Character 1 to look directly at the audience, humorously using a smirking facial expression to indicate that they cannot believe how ridiculous Character 2 is being.
   (c) *Scenario 3*: Working with the costume designer, I would have the wealthy character in a neatly pressed, expensive looking suit, whereas the poorer character will have a cheaper looking shirt and trousers and no tie.

31. Purpose

1 **(a)** The purpose of the play is to **question** – **(iii)** The play presents the audience with the consequences of different actions, encouraging them to query things around them.
   (b) The purpose of the play is to **challenge** – **(i)** The play encourages the audience to dispute and question situations and people in power.
   (c) The purpose of the play is to **educate** – **(vii)** The play engages the audience at a deep level and teaches them about issues and situations.
   (d) The purpose of the play is to **entertain** – **(ii)** The play provides the audience with an escape from the stresses of everyday life.
   (e) The purpose of the play is to **empower** – **(vi)** The play shows the audience how people can make a real difference and demonstrates how they might go about changing things.
   (f) The purpose of the play is to **influence** – **(iv)** The play encourages the audience to look at different perspectives and tries to shape their opinion.
   (g) The purpose of the play is to **encourage understanding** – **(v)** The play encourages the audience to think about the characters and issues and to develop empathy and understanding of the situation.
2 This example answer is based on *Government Inspector*:
   (a) Name of performance text: *Government Inspector*
   The purpose of my performance text: to educate and inform the audience and to challenge them to ask questions.
   (b) Concept map showing evidence of purpose for *Government Inspector*:
   - The play was written at a time of serious political corruption in Russia (to inform).
   - The play uses humour and satire to poke fun at political officials (to entertain).

- The play highlights that corruption was accepted by many in power as normal behaviour (to challenge).
- The play tells the wider public about these issues (to inform).

32. Managing the audience

1 *Perspective*: A director may choose to give the audience a greater <u>view</u> of the action than some characters in the play. This can give the audience a wider <u>perspective</u> as to what is going on and enable them to put the action into a better <u>context</u>.

Purpose: A director being clear about the <u>purpose</u> of the play is vital. This is not just linked to comedy, but to all styles and <u>genres</u>. Clarity of purpose is important to performers, designers and the director, and can be a helpful tool in managing the audience <u>reaction</u>.

Climax: This is when the <u>action</u> builds up significant amounts of <u>tension</u>. When that tension reaches a <u>critical</u> point, it is then released, often suddenly and with explosive consequences.

Anticlimax: Similar to climax, the tension builds and is <u>released</u>. However, with anticlimax, the <u>resolution</u> is less explosive than expected, often leaving the audience feeling unfulfilled or with a sense of <u>disappointment</u>.

2 (a) To make the audience shocked, I would underscore the scene with dark and tension-filled music, creating an anxious atmosphere. The lighting would be low level and filled with dark blue and reds, leaving lots of shadows for the attacker to hide in. As Victoria falls, she becomes helpless. The attacker would then walk slowly and deliberately towards her, giving the audience time to think about what is about to happen.

(b) To make the audience laugh, I would use bright lighting to create a non-threatening atmosphere. As Victoria walks across the stage, she would stop to look in her handbag. This pattern would be repeated, with Victoria stopping several times; each time she stops, the young man would have to pretend to do something different. The fall, when it comes, is exaggerated and deliberate, allowing her to spring up in one jump and take up an aggressive karate position, frightening the young man away.

33. Choosing location and time

1 (a) To make the play relevant for a modern audience.

(b) To highlight a political or moral point about a contemporary issue.

(c) To modernise the original message that the playwright intended to convey and which might be lost when using the original setting.

(d) To bring the location into a local setting for the audience, bringing the action to them.

2 (a) To make a point regarding a historic issue.

(b) To indicate how the future may turn out if things do not change.

(c) To indicate that the issue is relevant to all time periods.

(d) To bring an issue up to date and make it more relevant to a modern audience.

3 This example answer is based on *An Inspector Calls*:

(a) Setting the play in the past:

- *Advantage 1*: It can provide an authentic setting, reflecting Britain in the final years before the First World War, when there was a clear social divide. This can then reflect the possibility that things have not changed as much as we (a modern-day audience) think.

- *Advantage 2*: The audience can be distanced from the action, enabling them to think about the issues objectively. They can question how each of the characters dealt with Eva and consider what they could have done differently. An audience can also consider what Eva could have done differently to help herself.

- *Disadvantage*: The audience may not make moral connections with their own lives as they may not identify with the extremes of the social divide presented in the play.

(b) Setting the play in the future:

- *Advantage 1*: The audience can see that the issue of moral responsibility is still relevant and that there remains a significant gap between the rich and poor.

- *Advantage 2*: The play can be updated for a younger audience, presenting the issues as directly impacting them in terms of employment rights and agencies who can support those facing financial hardships.

- *Disadvantage*: Modern society has more support for people who fall on hard times, which may make Eva Smith appear not to really want help.

34. Contexts

1 (a) Social context – this reflects what is happening to ordinary people at the time the play is set.

(b) Historical context – this reflects the important historical events happening at the time the play is set.

(c) Cultural context – this reflects the shared sense of identity that different sections of society have at the time the play is set.

2 Play A:

(a) Contexts:

(i) *Social*: Many women were worried about the welfare of children who had been evacuated and male relatives who had been sent to fight, and yet they were working in a munitions factory, making weapons that will kill and maim other people.

(ii) *Historical*: The Second World War had a huge impact on all aspects of life in Britain and having women making weapons in a factory was an important – and, at that time, unusual – part of the war effort.

(iii) *Cultural*: During this time, Britain and its allies saw themselves as being on the side of 'good', fighting against the 'evil' Nazi regime.

(b) Influence on my interpretation as director:

(i) *Social*: Many of the characters suffer mixed emotions, such as pride (they are supporting the war effort and making a contribution) mixed with guilt (they are creating weapons that will kill the loved ones of others). There will be a strong sense of community as many of the characters will share similar experiences. The cast must be able to communicate to the audience a sense of a community thrown together by war.

(ii) *Historical*: Costumes, set, props and other design aspects must reflect the appropriate time period. This may include personal props, such as wristwatches, as well as hairstyles or even foodstuffs, which were rationed during the war years and therefore important indications of the era.

        (iii) *Cultural*: See 'social'; in this instance social and cultural aspects are closely linked.

Play B:

(a) Contexts:
    (i) *Social*: Ordinary people coming together to fight against racism and inequality.
    (ii) *Historical*: The struggle against apartheid was an important fight for human rights that continued for many years.
    (iii) *Cultural*: Black people have been oppressed by white people in many ways throughout modern history, including slavery. Apartheid is a more modern example of this oppression.

(b) Influence on my interpretation as director:
    (i) *Social*: This performance must highlight the importance of making a stand against 'inequality', driving people to stand up to and challenge problems when they arise.
    (ii) *Historical*: Black South Africans suffered cruel and inhumane treatment under the apartheid regime. The play should include various reminders of this, such as signs of the black people's poverty and intolerable living conditions, and the tendency of the white South Africans to respond with violence and intimidation.
    (iii) *Cultural*: The production should reflect the cultural and racial identity of the people involved, highlighting the humanity of those who are being oppressed and the inhumanity of the oppressors, demonstrating that all forms of racism are deeply harmful to the human spirit. It should also convey the message that the human spirit is to be admired when it can rise to challenge such injustices, despite the fear of violent retaliation and the risk of loss (of loved ones).

35. Mood and atmosphere

1 Mood is the term used to describe how a scene or moment within a production makes the audience feel. It has strong links to the emotions being communicated to the audience. Mood is often created by different theatrical elements working together. Some of these elements include vision, message, location and the context of the performance.
   Atmosphere is similar to mood, but it is more closely linked to the emotions of the audience. Therefore, the atmosphere can be considered to be what the audience feels as a result of the mood of the scene.

2 (a) Costume can create a humorous atmosphere in numerous ways. If a costume is deliberately too big or too small, this can have a significant impact on the way the character moves. For example, if it is too tight, it may make the character have difficulty walking. Similarly, if the costume is too big, the character may be constantly tripping up or having to gather the costume together before moving. Colours used for costumes can also have a strong impact. If bright, primary colours are used, particularly if they clash, this can add to any comedy moments. A good example of this is the bright yellow stockings worn by the humourless Malvolio in *Twelfth Night*. This clash between the personality of the character and the costume worn creates humour for the audience, making the character appear ridiculous.

(b) A simple, symbolic set can create a mysterious atmosphere, making the audience imagine what is there rather than making it explicit. For example, a performer can use a single doorway to indicate something fearful on the other side. This would be effective using an 'end-on' stage, as the audience would not be able to see beyond the door. Equally, a set that obscures the view of some parts of the stage for the audience can be mysterious. This is because some of the action can be implied to take place beyond the view of the audience, forcing them to fill in the unknown with their own imagination. For example, by including an object that is either out of context or difficult to interpret, you can provoke the audience to think and ask questions.

36. Style

1 (a) Naturalistic style:
    (i) *Set*: *Feature 1*: Set looks like the real location of the scene. *Feature 2*: Set is highly detailed. *Example*: A scene set in a wood may use an assortment of trees; the floor may be covered in fallen leaves.
    (ii) *Costume*: *Feature 1*: Costumes look like the characters' real clothes. *Feature 2*: Costumes convey information such as status. *Example*: A 17th-century executioner would wear a sleeveless shirt and mask.
    (iii) *Lighting*: *Feature 1*: Lighting realistically shows the time of day or location. *Feature 2*: Light is distributed realistically. *Example*: A scene set in a moonlit field would use a pale, silver light, covering the space evenly.

(b) Abstract style:
    (i) *Set*: *Feature 1*: Set represents the location using symbolism. *Feature 2*: Set may represent more than one place. *Example*: Wooden planks can represent trees in a wood. The planks can be rearranged and moved to represent something different, such as a building.
    (ii) *Costume*: *Feature 1*: Costumes represent the types of character. *Feature 2*: Costumes include symbolic information. *Example*: A 17th-century executioner may be shown wearing all black, embroidered with a skull (to symbolise death).
    (iii) *Lighting*: *Feature 1*: Lighting represents the location or situation. *Feature 2*: Lighting may convey emotions. *Example*: A scene set in a moonlit field may have bright spotlights on the backdrop and centre stage, symbolising the moon. The rest of the stage could be washed in blue light.

2 Figure 1: Abstract; Figure 2: Naturalistic

37. Presenting location and time

1 (a) Hospital:
    (i) Modern hospital bed linked to electronic monitor. Sound effect of monitor beeping. Bed surrounded by mobile privacy screen.
    (ii) Single metal bed. White screen, filling rear of stage, pulled taut with projection of large red cross. Sound effects of emergency siren and flashing red and blue lights introduce the beginning of the scene.

(b) Mechanic's garage:
    (i) Metallic, treaded floor (non-slip). Sound effect of cars being revved and clanking of tools being used and replaced. Large tool chest, filled with real tools.

(ii) Three piles of tyres, stacked flat on top of each other. Large spanner emblem suspended on rear backdrop. Mixed sound effects, including engines and metal clash, arranged rhythmically with drumbeat to create underscoring and symbolic soundtrack.

2 (a) 1540:
   (i) *Office*: Old-fashioned desk and chair. Quill and parchment. Candle.
   (ii) *Street*: Backdrop of Tudor houses. Floor is cobbled street. Shop signs reflect Tudor signs (such as images of keys or fish to indicate what is sold).
   (iii) *Prison cell*: Large grey stone backdrop. Lit by flaming lamp. Straw and wooden bench. Sound effect of water dripping.
 (b) Present:
   (i) *Office*: Desktop computer and screen. Open plan. Plastic swivel chairs.
   (ii) *Street*: Contemporary car in background. Backdrop of modern block of flats. Sound effects of vehicles with petrol or diesel engines passing by.
   (iii) *Prison cell*: Metal bed. Background sound effects of prisoners talking or shouting and metal door slamming.
 (c) 2150:
   (i) *Office*: Bright lighting. Futuristic moulded plastic chair. Transparent touch screen instead of desktop computer.
   (ii) *Street*: Futuristic backdrop of bright, clean buildings. Road indicated by LED strip lights. Vehicle sound effects represented by 'swoosh' noises to indicate an alternative fuel to petrol or diesel engines.
   (iii) *Prison cell*: Glass cylindrical cell. Single bed in centre of tube. Harsh, stark lighting.

38. Staging and blocking

1

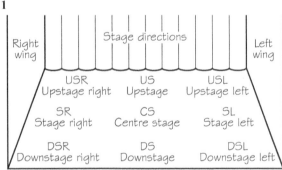

2 (a) Stage plan A: Proscenium arch:
   • Problem: Performer A is hidden behind the stage flat.
   • Solution: Bring Performer A in front of the stage flat.
 (b) Stage plan B: Theatre-in-the-round:
   • Problem: All the performers are facing the same way, putting their backs to some of the audience.
   • Solution: Move the performers so they are facing different directions and include all of the audience.
 (c) Stage plan C: Traverse theatre:
   • Problem: The stage flat blocks the view of half of the stage.

• Solution: Remove the stage flat to create a clear view of all of the stage.

39. Stage business, relationships and proxemics

1 (a) The man nervously plays with a ring on his finger, spinning it around and around.
 (b) The shop owner takes a small offcut from a cotton sheet and twists it around her hand, pulling it taut before releasing it.
 (c) A muffled laugh bursts through the young woman's clenched mouth before she takes a handkerchief and holds it over her mouth.

2 For example:
(a) Proscenium arch stage: A and B are downstage, facing out over the audience in different directions – not wanting to look at each other.

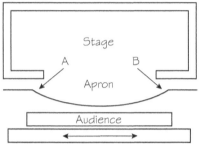

(b) Theatre-in-the-round: A is on bended knee, facing B. A is positioned just to the right of centre stage. B, positioned slightly upstage, is looking in the opposite direction.

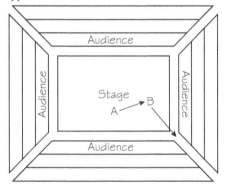

40. Characterisation and style

1 • Who are they? What sort of person are they?
  • Where has the character come from – both physically and emotionally?
  • Is the character comic or serious?
  • What is the purpose or function of the character within the play? What do they want to achieve?

2 (a) Delivered with sarcasm and anger. Emphasis on 'you' and 'important'. Looks directly at the other characters with hatred and anger as he is being physically dragged below a group of people who represent a society with higher status than him.
 (b) Delivered with hope and nervousness. Emphasis on 'companion'. During the line, moves closer to the other character, keeping them in full eye contact at all times. A slight smile and raised eyebrow, indicating openness.
 (c) Delivered with pity and dislike. Emphasis on 'difference' and 'own benefit'. Begins the line by looking at the other character but then shakes his head and turns away with disgust. The staging on which the character stands begins to rise, lifting the character higher above the others, symbolising his moral superiority.

Designer: costume
41. The costume designer

1 A costume designer designs the costumes for a production. They work with the <u>director</u> to create costumes that are <u>consistent</u> with the chosen <u>style</u> and characterisation. The costume designer will carry out <u>research</u> to ensure the designs are accurate from a range of different perspectives, such as <u>social</u>, cultural or <u>historical</u>. They will also consider how costume can help to convey key themes and messages to an <u>audience</u>. The costume designer will produce initial ideas, then develop them into a final design. Finally, the costume designer will work with the <u>performers</u> to ensure the fit and style are appropriate.

2 *Primary responsibility of the director*: Creating an overall vision for the performance.
Primary responsibility of the designer: Producing final costume designs; Representing the themes and issues of the play through costume; Working with the performers to ensure the costumes are practical and safe to use on stage.

3 As a costume designer, I would research the era to ensure the costumes reflect what a young servant girl in a large townhouse would wear. This would also support the naturalistic style. Both girls would wear full-length black dresses with long, tight sleeves. They would also wear a long white apron. However, Elizabeth's apron would be clean, showing the audience that she is trying to distance herself from the situation, while Karen's apron would be dirty and slightly ripped near the shoulder strap to indicate to the audience that she is deeply involved in whatever the situation is. The difference in the costumes would make the audience question what the problem is. It would also give Karen a reason to be extra nervous, as her appearance would instantly cause someone to ask questions as to how she became like that in the first place, adding tension for the audience.

42. Costume and context

1 (a) *Love*: The costume could be mainly red, a colour linked with love and passion. Small red hearts could be included in the pattern of a costume for a character who is in love with another.
   (b) Hate: A character who is hateful could wear thick, heavy clothing, reflective of a bad mood. The main colour could be black – again, to reflect the mood of the character.
   (c) Wealth: A wealthy character could wear stylish, well-fitting clothes to indicate they have been individually tailored. The quality of the material would be high and accessorised with expensive items, such as gold buttons or jewelled cufflinks.
   (d) A cold winter: A character living in a cold environment could wear a heavy coat, scarf and gloves. Under the coat would be a thick woollen jumper. Heavy boots or wellingtons could also indicate the presence of cold and snow.

2 Descriptions/costume sketches might include, for example:
   (a) The officer would be wearing the full military dress uniform, complete with medals previously awarded, to indicate that this is a formal occasion where there is an expectation of what should be worn. The uniform, which is clean, immaculately ironed and spotless, would indicate the character's role in the military, and the medals would provide the context

– that this is a character who is brave and used to putting themselves in danger. The modern style of the uniform would help the audience understand the play is set in the present day.
   (b) The prisoner would be wearing his own clothes to show that the play is set in the past (before the days when prisoners were issued prison uniforms). However, they will be filthy to show the conditions he has been kept in. They will also be ripped to show that he has been there a long time and that his well-being and appearance has not been cared for by his captors. Additionally, the clothes will be baggy on him because he has lost weight due to malnourishment and illness during his imprisonment.

43. Aspects of costume

1 • Accessories – for example, handbag, mobile phone
   • Masks – for example, full mask or half mask
   • Make-up – for example, foundation or lipstick
   • Hair – for example, 1960s beehive hairstyle or dyed hair
2 • Accessories: handkerchief, bag, watch, mobile phone, walking stick, hat
   • Masks: masquerade, half mask, full mask, fixed expression
   • Make-up: foundation, blusher, eyeliner, lipstick, face paint
   • Hair: wig, cropped, gel, hairspray, greying
   • Materials: cotton, leather, plastic, metal
   • Practicality: lightweight, cool, flexible, does not make noise

44. Materials and colours

1 • Wood: Advantage: strong; Disadvantage: can be hot under the lights
   • Lace: Advantage: enhances intricate costume; Disadvantage: can be hard to see from a distance
   • Metal: Advantage: can provide an authentic look; Disadvantage: can be noisy
   • Plastic/PVC: Advantage: a lightweight alternative to leather; Disadvantage: not breathable so can be hot under lighting
   • Cotton: Advantage: easy to dye or alter; Disadvantage: can rip easily
   • Leather: Advantage: can look very authentic; Disadvantage: can be hot under stage lighting
   • Velvet: Advantage: can look luxurious for high-status characters; Disadvantage: can be expensive
2 *Character A*: The main costume will be black to signify the role of the character (a religious minister). Black also indicates high status. A white neck collar would signify purity and represent the religious position of the character.
   Character B: Pink leggings would communicate the character's naivety and innocence, as well as providing a link back to her childhood that is rapidly disappearing. A colourful top, mixed with yellow and blue, would indicate her youth and joy, mixed with truthfulness. A red hairband would then indicate the danger the character is facing.
   Character C: To show her innocence, the main costume colour is a dazzling white. This also indicates her purity and childlike nature, and how she has been protected from the problems of the world. However, to show that she is not entirely isolated from her actions, a red sash around her waist, built into the costume, could indicate her negative impact on others.

45. Accessories and masks

1 *Character A*: His accessory would be a diamond-encrusted sword, worn in an open scabbard. The sword would be ceremonial, rather than a serious weapon, but the diamonds would show that he is a man of wealth, whereas the sword would represent his power. The open scabbard would ensure it is fully on display to the people in the city as well as the audience.

Character B: His accessory would be a gold pocket watch, kept in his pocket and worn on a gold chain that is always on display. The pocket watch would be from the time period. It would allow the performer to constantly keep looking at it, in order to show that he considers his time valuable.

Character C: Her accessory could be a branded sports rucksack. This would carry things such as her schoolbooks, as well as small items such as a mobile phone, make-up, purse and so on. The branded bag would indicate that she is fashion conscious, especially in front of her friends.

Character D: His accessory could be a high-quality top hat with a velvet covering to indicate his wealth and status. It would also be well brushed and cared for, which would indicate that he has very high standards.

2 • To give a character anonymity – for example, masks can be worn to hide their identity from other characters or the audience.
  • To provide a contrast from other characters – for example, a group of performers could wear masks to show the audience they are the chorus in a Greek play.
  • To represent a non-human character – for example, if performers have to portray animals, masks can be a very effective way to visually communicate this.

46. Make-up and hair

1 (a) Abstract; the make-up depicts a non-human character.
  (b) Naturalistic; although slightly exaggerated, this is a style of make-up a gothic teenager may wear in reality.
  (c) Naturalistic; the make-up simply enhances the natural features of Elizabeth's face and suggests someone who is hard-working and careworn, and who has little money or time to spend on her appearance.
  (d) Abstract; the make-up is heavy and makes the person look like a god or as though they are wearing a mask – slightly unreal.

2 (a) Her hair will show the fashion of the time, which was to pile up hair at the front and on top of the head and wear a jewelled fascinator. Her hair will be going grey but is immaculately cared for and styled.
  (b) Bald on top but with some hair on the sides and back. The hair that is present is short, indicating an attempt to maintain standards, and greying (to show the stress he is under).
  (c) Long hair with streaks of colour. Her hair is unstyled and messy to show that she does not really care for her appearance. The hair needs to be held or tied back to ensure it does not obscure her face.
  (d) Oiled or waxed hair, parted to the side, as was the fashion in 1896. The hair is quite short and full of colour. Narrow sideburns, neatly trimmed, which also reflect the trend at the end of the late Victorian period.

47. Practicality and safety

1 Any three from:
  • Weight – the costume should not be too heavy for the performer to use.
  • Noise – the costume should not be too noisy as this will distract the audience.
  • Vision – the costume should give the performer a clear field of vision.
  • Movement – the costume should allow the performer to move and speak freely.
  • Heat – the costume should prevent the performer from getting too hot under the stage lights.

2 (a) Aluminium chainmail – reflects the time period; aluminium is lighter than tradition metals and will make less noise when the performer moves.
  (b) PVC jerkin – PVC is lighter than leather and is also cooler, which will make the performer more comfortable under the stage lights.
  (c) Cotton shirt – the costume needs to be wet to show the bad weather, and cotton is lighter and more comfortable than wool when wet. It is also easier to rip and stain, which will help to show the arm wound.

3 Possible answers include:
  (a) *Potential hazards*: Audience members could step on the dress, causing it to tear or the performer to trip. Tripping over when climbing steps. *Possible solutions*: Pinning the dress to keep it away from the audience. Shortening the dress / providing a method for the performer to hitch up the dress.
  (b) *Potential hazards*: Candles could burn / set fire to costume. The performers could knock over candles if the costume is too flowing and not able to be controlled by the performer. *Possible solutions*: Ensure all costumes are made from flame-retardant material / treated to be flame retardant. Ensure the performers can hold the costumes and all movements are controlled, safely and securely.

Designer: lighting
48. The lighting designer

1 A lighting designer designs the stage lighting for a production. The lighting designer works with the director to create a detailed lighting design that reflects the themes and issues selected by the director. Once the general style has been agreed, the lighting designer will consider how lighting can help to convey important information and highlight key moments to an audience. From this point, the lighting designer will produce initial ideas, which will then be developed and refined until a final design is produced. The lighting designer may also supervise the rigging and programming of the lights as the design is finalised.

2 *Primary responsibility of the director*: Creating an overall vision for the performance.
Primary responsibility of the lighting designer: Producing final lighting designs; Representing the themes and issues of the play through the lighting; Working with members of the production crew to rig and programme the lighting desk to ensure the lighting reflects the intended design.

3 As a lighting designer, I would research the era to find out what sort of lighting would be available in a wealthy townhouse in 1862. As there would be no electricity, the characters could hold candles to indicate the time period to the audience. This would also highlight the fact they are sneaking around. To reinforce the light from the candles, which would not be enough to light

the stage, I would include a pale orange wash. From stage left, I would have a cold, pale blue or white light, representing the moonlight coming through a window. This would include a window frame gobo and be squared off using the shutters from inside the lamp to give the shape of a window. This light would illuminate centre stage – exactly where the box is positioned – and would therefore highlight the importance of the box and direct the audience's attention.

49. Colour, symbolism, mood and atmosphere

1 (a) The stage would be washed with bright, warm lighting, such as yellows and oranges. These would be symbolic of the joy and happiness of the couples getting together and provide the audience with a warm and safe feeling suggestive of a happy ending. This lighting would be enhanced with bright white light to indicate purity and joy.

(b) The atmosphere is one of fear and tension. Therefore, I would use a narrow-beamed red spotlight, angled from the side, to show the audience both the growing light of the dawn through the window, as well as to symbolise the fear the old man is feeling. I would also use a red spotlight on the soldier to highlight that he is dangerous. The rest of the stage would be in blackout to show the physical and symbolic distance between the characters.

(c) The stage would initially be filled with a blinding white light, to disorientate and confuse the audience. This could then be replaced with a bright white strobe effect but mixed with flashing red and blue lights, to indicate both the danger and also the police presence in the scene. This lighting, mixed with the alternating blackouts, will create a powerful and frightening atmosphere for the audience to experience.

2 (a) I would use a pale blue wash to symbolise night. As the characters move around the space, I would bathe the next character to be eliminated in a growing red light to symbolise both death and danger, and to indicate that they are about to meet their end.

(b) I would use a range of leaf gobos to give the audience the impression of light coming through leaves on trees. Different shades of light green – which give a calming, non-threatening atmosphere – would symbolise light reflecting from the leaves. A single, soft-edged, wide-beamed spotlight, also with a leaf gobo, would indicate the warmth and welcoming sunlight.

50. Style, location and era

1 (a) *Lighting style*: naturalistic
   Key features:
   - The lighting gives the impression that there is a single light source in the room (the lamp). It is brighter on the male performer, as he is closer to the light source than the female performer, who is further away.
   - There is no colour – only white – as you would have in a standard domestic household.
   - Blacked out windows and shadows above the fireplace help to indicate night.
   - Rear lighting provides a silhouette of the windows, helping to emphasise and reinforce the naturalistic set.

(b) *Lighting style*: abstract
   Key features:
   - A range of colours, including blue, white and yellow, are mixed in the set.
   - Lighting is the main design element, filling a near-empty stage.
   - The cluster of hanging light bulbs is symbolic of the power of light and electricity

2 (a) Lighting would include a lot of dark blues and washed-out grey lights to indicate the poor weather. As the scene progresses, the light would become gradually brighter to indicate that the scene takes place outside as the morning light grows.

(b) Lighting would be bright and quite harsh as it is utility lighting for a working building rather than lighting for comfort. There would be a slightly yellow hint to the lighting, representing the incandescent bulbs of the time, and the lighting levels would remain constant at all times to show it is artificial lighting indoors.

3 (a) At this time, candles or gaslight would have been the main source of lighting; this produces a yellow-coloured flame. Therefore, I would use a yellow wash with a flickering effect to represent the era.

(b) Modern electric domestic lighting produces an even and steady effect. I would therefore use a warm white light, representative of contemporary light bulbs, in an even stage wash to light the whole of the set.

51. Types of lantern

1 (a) Soft-edged spotlight – (ii) Generally easy to blend into other types of lighting used in the design. Can be used to light or highlight specific areas in the performance area.

(b) Profile spotlight – (iv) Sharp and clearly defined edge. Excellent when lighting precise spots in a performance area.

(c) Floodlight – (i) Gives a lot of light to a wide area on the stage. Very helpful when providing general lighting to large stage areas.

(d) Parcan – (iii) Narrower focus than a flood but a very versatile lamp. Can be used for lighting large areas in colour.

2 (a) Initially, I would have the whole stage lit evenly, using floodlights, to show that the whole area is equally important. However, once the mobile phone has been placed, I would then use soft-edged spotlights to indicate the areas on stage where the group of friends have hidden themselves. As the bully walks on, I would highlight the phone with a hard-edged profile spotlight to direct the audience's attention to the fact that the bully has seen the mobile. As he picks it up, the profile spot fades out and the soft-edged spotlights upstage are then emphasised, again to direct attention on the reactions of the group of friends.

(b) The first thing the lights must do is to indicate that it is night-time. This can be done with a dark blue wash across the stage, with a small, pale yellow, soft-edged spotlight on the face of the old man. To highlight the entrance of the spirit, I would then bring up a green wash from where he comes on stage. The doors appear upstage. As the spirit talks about the three doors, all three could be highlighted, each with a different colour, but initially at the same level of intensity. As the spirit tells the old man about what is behind each specific door, the intensity of the light would rise on that specific door and diminish on the other two doors.

52. Lighting angles

1 Figure 1: Sidelight; Figure 2: Backlight

2 (a) High front light:
- Features: It provides a clear and natural light (similar to the sun or light bulbs). It provides general lighting of the stage from above and in front of the performers.
- Uses: It helps the audience see what is happening on stage. It prevents performers or the audience from being blinded by the light. It is the most often used angle of lighting.

(b) Backlight:
- Features: Placed behind the action, the light will face the audience, often providing depth or obscuring some of the finer details on stage. It can add a sense of mystery.
- Uses: Very often, the detailed features of the performer or staging can be obscured by shadow and this can be very helpful in creating a tense or mysterious atmosphere for the audience. It can also imply morning or evening, where a low sun often reduces visual clarity.

(c) Up-light:
- Features: Placed below the performers, the light is projected upwards, creating a range of different types of shadows on both performers and objects. It can add suspense or tension.
- Uses: Shadows produced on the face give a skeletal impression and so uplighting can be very useful in a horror scene.

(d) Sidelight:
- Features: Often placed in the wings of stages, sidelights tend to be at the same height as objects or performers on stage. They can produce an abstract effect or represent a specific event or location.
- Uses: Sidelights can help to direct the audience's attention to specific areas on stage. For example, a sidelight may represent a door being opened and light flooding in, or a vehicle approaching with the lights on full.

53. Gels, barn doors and gobos

1 (a) A gel is a sheet of coloured plastic that is placed in front of a lamp (using a gel holder) in order to change the colour of the light produced.

(b) A colour changer is a device that contains a roll of different coloured gels. It is placed in front of a lamp and can be remotely controlled to enable one lamp to produce a range of different colours.

(c) Barn doors are hinged, metal shutters that can be positioned to block light from reaching a certain part of the performance area.

(d) A gobo is a small disc, usually made of metal, which is cut into specific shapes and patterns. These patterns or shapes are then placed in front of a lamp and projected onto the performance area.

2 (a) *Prison*: Prison bars

(b) *Tropical island*: Palm trees

(c) *Woodland*: Leaves effect

(d) *Church*: Large, arched stained-glass window

(e) *Night-time*: Stars-and-moon effect

(f) *Winter*: Snowflakes effect

3 I would use a gobo of barbed wire across the middle of the stage to show that there is a physical divide between the two characters. As the wall is built, this can then be replaced by a gobo of a solid wall. I would also use a colour changer to change the light representing East Germany from bright warm colours to darker, colder pale blues and white, emphasising to the audience the stark contrast between east and west.

54. Structure and focus

1 (a) True

(b) False. Blackout is where the lights all go out at once. It can be used to signal important moments in the performance. This might include the start of the performance, when the house lights dim to indicate to the audience that the performance is about to start. Equally, it may be at the end of the performance, to show that the performance has finished. Blackouts may also be used at key moments of the performance to create tension.

(c) True

(d) False. Snap is where the lighting suddenly changes from one lighting state to another. This can be useful to create tension or to indicate a very sudden change in character behaviour (for example, a performer directly addressing the audience and then 'going back' into the scene).

(e) True

(f) True

2 (a) Fade to blackout

(b) Cross fade between the two scenes

(c) Snap

3 To create maximum impact, I would use a snap between both sides of the stage. While the man is calmly explaining, the torture scene would be in blackout; while the torture scene is active, the other side of the stage would be in blackout. This use of blackout would ensure the audience's focus remains firmly on the 'active' part of the stage.

Designer: set
55. The set designer

1 A set designer creates the physical location on stage. This conveys setting, and key themes and messages, to the audience. A set designer works with the director to establish what the set should communicate and to ensure there is consistency with other design elements. They develop initial ideas to create an appropriate space, including a range of entrances and exits, and possibly different levels. They then work with the construction team to ensure the set is realised as practically and as closely as possible to the original design.

2 *Primary responsibility of the director*: Organising the rehearsal schedule
Primary responsibility of the set designer: Working with members of the construction crew to build and realise a set that reflects the intended design; Producing final set designs; Representing the themes and issues of the play through the set.

3 As a set designer, the first thing I would need to do is ensure that the location is properly represented. The room is a bedroom in 1862. I would have a single bed – a metal tube design to reflect the time. The bed would be neatly made up using non-fitted sheets and a blanket with one white pillow. It would be positioned upstage

right so as not to get in the way of the performers or distract the audience but to indicate the time. Next to the bed would be a plain bedside table. The majority of the space would be empty. However, because the style is naturalistic, I would have the flooring made of traditional floorboards (again, to represent the time) with a small, patterned rug in the centre. To direct the attention of the audience, I would place the box on this rug, creating a focal point.

56. Style and genre

1 (a) *Style*: Naturalistic; *How I can tell*: The doors and furniture are realistic and look like items that would actually be found in this location.

(b) *Style*: Abstract; *How I can tell*: Bright colours and exaggerated openings in the hedge mean this is not a realistic hedge.

2 As a set designer, the first thing to consider is exactly how to integrate the different positions required by the director and performers into the set. Once these exact positions have been established, I would then look at creating the different routes and levels required to get to those locations. This could include using hand holds built into the flats or walls, or using reinforced furniture to enable the performers to climb up using those. The set would need to have a ceiling area that contained bars, or holding areas from which the performers could be suspended. Finally, all of the set would need to be secured to ensure the health and safety of all of the cast and crew before, during and after the performance.

57. Colours, location and time

1 (a) To emphasise the location as an orchard, I would mainly use brown and green to indicate a large number of trees. To reflect the emotions of the lovers and the fact that they are risking being caught, I would paint the bench upon which they sit red, symbolising the love and passion they have for each other, as well as the danger they may be in.

(b) The main colours here should be white and browns. The white would be used on the walls to signify how the stone had been plastered and painted. The white also represents purity and innocence, which is important for the symbolism of religion, and would be a prominent part of the building as it is a chapel for the community. The furniture and flooring would be dark brown to show that wood was the main building material of the time. Brown also represents the earth and nature, which reflects the agricultural nature of the community.

(c) The floor covering would be a rich red colour, symbolising how the Mayor has squeezed the life from the community for his own gain. The chairs would be a 19th-century style – solid, with highly polished dark-brown wood and edged with gold leaf; this will represent the money the Mayor has lavished on his office. The cushions on the chairs would be purple, to represent the regal status the Mayor wants to have.

2 (a) *A dining room in 1600*: Exposed, grey stone walls with colourful woollen tapestries hanging down.

(b) *A dining room in 1912*: Smooth walls, covered in fine wallpaper. Fine art landscapes hang from the walls in grand frames.

(c) *A rustic dining table in 1692*: The table would be large and solid. The wood would be untreated and bare.

(d) *A dining table in 2008*: The table would be made of metal and glass, held together with modern screw fixings.

58. Practicality, health and safety

1 (a) Use of space; it should be simple for a performer to reach different parts of the performance area quickly and safely.

(b) Trip hazards; the performers should be able to move around the space without fear of falling over.

(c) Levels; the height of any steps or levels should not cause the performer to struggle between the different levels (unless it is a specific requirement for them to do so!).

(d) Portability; if the production is touring, the set needs to be able to be transported to different locations.

(e) Flexibility; if the production is touring, the set will need to work in a variety of different locations and staging styles.

(f) Construction; if the set needs to be constructed and dismantled regularly for a touring company, this needs to be a relatively quick and simple task in order to save time and money.

2 (a) *Potential hazards*: Falling when running. Bumping into furniture. Tripping over when climbing steps. *Possible solutions*: Ensure there is sufficient space between stage furniture. Non-slip floor covering. Ensure solid construction of spiral staircase with handrails. Balcony to have secure railings around.

(b) *Potential hazards*: Candles could burn / set fire to set. Candles could be knocked over. *Possible solutions*: Ensure all set is treated to be flame retardant. Ensure the table is smooth and not covered with unnecessary props, thereby enabling the lamps to be put in a safe location away from the edge of the table.

(c) *Potential hazards*: The table could be heavy and cause injury when lifted. It could cause a blockage when off stage. *Possible solutions*: Ensure the wood is made of lightweight materials and then painted to look like heavy wood. Put table on caster wheels to make it easier to manoeuvre. Ensure there is a specific and dedicated space to store the table when it is off stage.

59. Props and stage furniture

1 (a) Stage flat – scenery; (b) Handkerchief – personal prop; (c) Mobile phone – personal prop; (d) Table – stage furniture; (e) Landline telephone – stage furniture; (f) Umbrella – personal prop; (g) Staircase – scenery; (h) Desk lamp – stage furniture

2 (a) A small metal trolley on which the woman places dirty cutlery and crockery; a cloth for wiping tables in a pocket of her apron.

(b) A small stack of hard-backed books; a small leather bag containing papers; a pen and inkwell to enable her to make notes.

(c) An elaborately decorated sword to show status and power; a small money pouch with gold coins to symbolise wealth.

(d) An early design stethoscope – similar to an ear trumpet – to represent the medical profession and to show that modern examples had not reached the remote town at this point.

60. Levels, entrances and exits

1 (a) Power – If a character is raised above others, the levels could show that this character has more power

than the others. Alternatively, if a character is placed lower than others, it may show they have less power than those placed above them.

(b) Status – Status is similar to power, but is more about how a character is viewed by others rather than the amount of control a character has over others. A higher status can be shown through a raised level and a lower status through a lower level.

(c) Perspective – Raising a character up above the action can suggest to an audience that this character has a wider view of the action. This character might be able to make connections between events or see the reasons behind why something is happening, whereas a character in the middle of the action may miss something that is about to happen.

(d) Variation – Using a range of different levels can create visual interest for the audience. If everything were staged on the same level, the performance might become dull and lack variety. Using different levels (including decisions about whether a character should sit or lie down, for example) helps to add variety to the set and the production.

2 (a) Upstage centre (USC): To suggest that the character entering here is very important, with everyone turning to see them enter.

(b) Downstage left (DSL): This could lead to a specific area or location, and might only be used for the purpose of going to that particular location.

(c) Through the audience: To take the action into the audience and make the audience feel an integrated part of the performance.

61. Types of staging and terminology

1 A: Downstage centre; B: Upstage left; C: Centre stage; D: Downstage right

2 (a) *Staging style*: Theatre-in-the-round. *Advantage*: The audience gets a 360-degree view of the stage. *Disadvantage*: Blocking and sightlines can be difficult for some audience members when performers have their backs to them.

(b) *Staging style*: Traverse theatre. *Advantage*: This style can be very intimate for the audience and performers. *Disadvantage*: It can be difficult to use a large set and scenery as this can block the audience's view.

(c) *Staging style*: Thrust stage. *Advantage*: This style can bring the audience close to the action while still providing an area for a backdrop and scenery. *Disadvantage*: Sightlines can be a problem for the audience if the scene is not blocked correctly.

62. Symbolism, semiotics, spatial consideration and depth

1 (a) I would have a series of patterned curtains at the back of the stage, which could be drawn at the start of each scene and used to represent different locations – for example, comfortable curtains for home and clinical curtains for the hospital. Each curtain could include symbolic patterns, such as the outline of a wall for frustration, indicating that the characters are constantly trying to break down barriers.

(b) The young woman and her family are metaphorically going around in circles and therefore keep ending up where they started from. To show this, I would include circles within the set. This would include circles on the floor of the set where the outline of the circles change colour as the scene progresses. This could be achieved by either using lights or projection. However, as the young woman

finds herself 'back where she started', the colour will drain away back to the original colour, showing that no progress has been made.

2 (a)

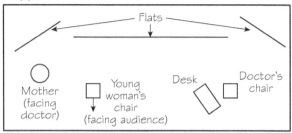

- Lots of space between chairs and desk.
- Chairs and desk downstage to give space in front of flats
- The flats (all upstage) can be covered with curtains, which can be pulled across to represent different locations.

(b) Depth can be used to help reinforce the frustration felt by the family. Upstage centre could be a door which, when opened, could reveal what appears to be a long corridor, stretching away from the young woman and symbolising the long journey she needs to take in order to get better.

Designer: sound
63. The sound designer

1 A sound designer designs the sound effects and music for a production. They work with the director to create a sound design that reflects the chosen style and helps to communicate key ideas, themes and emotions to an audience, as well as locations and time periods. The sound designer will read the text to understand what exactly is required from the sound (for example, what music is needed, and why). Initial ideas are developed into a final design. The sound designer may then work with musicians and technicians to supervise the recording, editing and production of the sound effects or music.

2 *Primary responsibility of the director*: Working with a team of designers to create a consistent design approach for the overall production.
Primary responsibility of the sound designer: Producing final sound designs; Representing the themes and issues of the play through the sound and music; Working with the production crew to prepare sound effects in preparation for the final performance.

3 As a sound designer, the two things I would want to really bring out for the audience in this scene is the atmosphere and the fact it is night-time. To do this, I would have an owl sound effect which, when combined with the lighting design elements, would clearly indicate to an audience that the scene is taking place at night. This effect would also have an impact on the atmosphere I am trying to create, as owls are often associated with an eerie, haunting atmosphere. I would also use the sound effect of a creaking floorboard. However, I would be careful to make this quite naturalistic, as if it were too loud or stereotyped it could cause the audience to laugh. Finally, after Elizabeth has left, I would use low music with a sense of building tension to develop the eerie atmosphere and make the audience feel on edge.

64. Music and sound effects

1 (a) Advantages:
(i) The sound effects/music could be fully integrated into the performance, blending in smoothly and adapting to the performer's specific performance that day/the live action on stage.

(ii) Hearing live music during a production adds to the audience's experience of the play and their overall enjoyment.

(iii) The sound effects/music can be much more authentic and have a greater quality than when using sound reproduction equipment.

(b) Disadvantages:

(i) Each performance of live music is different, which may cause inconsistency in the production as a whole.

(ii) Playing music live may place performers under increased pressure and strain.

(iii) There may be a need for extra crew or performers, as well as additional specialised equipment or instruments, adding to the cost of the overall production.

2 (a) The sound effects should be of the trap door of the gallows being suddenly opened, followed almost immediately by the short sound of bones being broken, ending with the sound of the creaking of a rope pulled taut.

(b) I would want to try to build up as much tension as possible, so I would use the sound effect of a slowly ticking clock. This would indicate that it seems time is passing slowly, drawing out the family's agony of having to wait.

65. Atmosphere and time

1 (a) Fear-filled:
- *Sound effects*: Heartbeat, gradually getting quicker. Creaking doors opening. Sudden scream.
- *Music*: Quiet, sustained music that builds up to a crescendo. Low-pitched notes played on stringed instruments.

(b) Joyous:
- *Sound effects*: Laughter. Party sound effects.
- *Music*: Light, dance-like music with a moderate volume and moderate-to-high tempo.

(c) Comic:
- *Sound effects*: Exaggerated laughter. Comedy percussion sound effects, such as a hooter or cymbal if a character falls over.
- *Music*: Fast-paced music. Often syncopated rhythms. May include comedic percussion noises.

2 (a) To create the impression of a town in the 16th century, I would blend together the sounds of horses walking over cobbled stones with the sound of cartwheels being drawn behind them. I would also include the occasional whinnying of a horse, as this was the main mode of transport at the time. This would also communicate the 'business-like' atmosphere of people getting on with their daily lives.

(b) As the main mode of transport in a 21st-century town is a car, I would include the sounds of vehicles moving around. This would include buses as well as people talking in the background. This would help to reinforce the constantly busy atmosphere of modern living, where it is difficult to find privacy. All of these sound effects would need to be relatively quiet so as not to drown out the speech of the performers.

(c) I would use a military-style march to represent the presence of the state. This would be played loudly over any lengthy moments of torture, partly to drown out the screams of the character, allowing the audience to imagine the pain as well as reducing the physical burden of screaming for the performer, and also to represent the idea that there is no escape from the state. This would reinforce the oppressive and terrifying atmosphere in the scene.

66. Location and genre

1 Docks – Seagulls crying. The sound effect of the sea.
An orchard – Wind blowing in the trees. Birdsong.
A workplace canteen – Quiet hum of people talking. Crockery being knocked together.
A playground – Children laughing. Sound effect of a football being kicked.

2 (a) *Historical drama*: Music written from the time period in which the play is set could be played to reflect a more naturalistic approach to the performance. This music would use contemporary instruments from the period. For example, a play set in the early 17th century would use a harpsichord rather than a piano, which was not invented until the early 18th century.

(b) *Romantic comedy*: Light, positive music to reflect the happy and joyous events of the characters falling in love. The music would be harmonious and rhythmical – possibly dance-like. This music could then present an opportunity for actual dance or movement sequences to be used, which could support an abstract approach using physical theatre.

(c) *Political drama*: Unharmonious music could be used to indicate conflict between the characters through discordant notes. This symbolic use of music would then reflect a more abstract approach to the performance. The music would start off quietly but then crescendo to indicate the rising tension within a scene.

3 The example answer is based on the performance text *Blue Stockings*:
Genre of performance text: Historical drama
As the genre is historical drama, any music used in the production would be played on a piano. This was a very popular instrument at the time and would be relatively easy to use in performance (either live or recorded) as it only requires one musician. The style of the music from this time period varied and therefore would provide a wide range of options, from the very serious to the more light-hearted, to reflect the mood and atmosphere on stage.

67. Sound equipment and levels

1 (a) *Equipment*: Laptop. *How it can be used*: Can be used to edit, store and play music and sound effects.

(b) *Equipment*: Mixing desk. *How it can be used*: To blend together a range of sound sources, including music, sound effects and microphones. Enables control of volume and sound quality of individual devices or inputs.

(c) *Equipment*: CD player. *How it can be used*: A reliable way to store and play a range of music and sound effects, although it can become scratched and dirty (and stop working).

(d) *Equipment*: Speakers. *How it can be used*: An output device enabling the audience and performers to hear the music or sound effects.

(e) *Equipment*: MP3 player. *How it can be used*: A device that stores music and sound effects digitally. It can be very portable and produce high sound quality.

(f) *Equipment*: Amplifier. *How it can be used*: It allows the sound to fill large spaces without spoiling sound quality. It is connected to a mixing desk or player.

2 The audience may not be able to hear any dialogue from the performers.

3 The performers may not be able to hear any sound effects, which may be important for a cue.

4 I could position the speakers behind the audience and play sound effects to make it sound to the audience as though events were happening behind them.

PERFORMANCE TEXTS

68. *1984*: overview

1 **(a)** True; **(b)** True; **(c)** False (the first performance was at the Nottingham Playhouse); **(d)** False (the play is set in Airstrip One); **(e)** False (the play cross-cuts between time periods; the Voice states that it was impossible to pin the date down to within a year or two, while the Father says that 1984 was over 100 years ago); **(f)** True; **(g)** False (the Company discuss whether the events witnessed were real; Winston is released from captivity but troubled by false memories); **(h)** False (the play is structured as one continuous performance)

2 If I were directing this section, I would want to make Winston the focus of attention, as this would represent to the audience that the Company are referring to him. He represents the character they are considering from the book. I would place him downstage centre, initially under a spotlight, making him the only focus of attention. As the light increases in intensity, this would reveal the others all standing behind him but at some distance. They would make Winston the focus of their attention, but their slight distance from him would show the audience that they are separate from him.

3 *Play*: 1984
Scene: Winston and Julia are in bed, just before they are arrested.
Scene title: The arrest
Theme 1: Love
Ideas for establishing theme 1: As Winston speaks about the singing woman and Julia repeats Winston's name, they should be closely embracing, almost clinging to each other, as they know their relationship cannot last. The audience will view their closeness as representative of the deep emotions they have for each other.
Theme 2: Power
Ideas for establishing theme 2: Winston and Julia accept they will be arrested, demonstrating the power of the Party. However, despite this acceptance, the uniformed men still restrain Winston and put a bag over Julia's head in an act of unnecessary violence and over-aggression.

69. *1984*: plot

1 *Opening section*: A child from next door screams out loud that Winston is a Thought Criminal.
Middle section 1: Julia passes Winston a note and they agree to meet in the countryside, where they begin their love affair.
Middle section 2: Winston and Julia meet O'Brien, who claims to be part of the resistance movement. They agree to join the fight against Big Brother.
Closing section: Winston is tortured until he eventually betrays Julia.

2 **(a)** The unborn
(b) It is as though Winston is unsure whether what he is experiencing is real or imagined. This then raises questions as to when these events are taking place and if the audience – or Company – can really trust what is being shared.

3 **(a)** The destruction of words
(b) He is filled with guilt as he realises that he could have done something, although he is also aware that the Party is powerful and that any action he took would likely be ineffective.

4 **(a)** The Brotherhood
(b) This approach also has a psychological impact on Winston. O'Brien is treating him almost as a child that he is caring for and this, when combined with the intense pain, has a deeply unsettling effect on Winston's mind.

5 **(a)** Sometime before 2050.
(b) Set against a backdrop of state control, Winston Smith falls in love and begins to stand up against the system. When he meets the mysterious O'Brien, his plans take a dramatic change – but is this reality or fiction?

70. *An Inspector Calls*: overview

1 **(a)** True; **(b)** True; **(c)** False (the first performance took place in Moscow); **(d)** True; **(e)** False (the play is set in 1912, just before Titanic sailed on 10 April 1912); **(f)** True; **(g)** True; **(h)** False (the play is structured into three acts)

2 As a director, I would first ensure the Inspector has the highest status. His position (indicated in the stage directions as 'in front of the door') would be upstage centre, allowing him to look down on the two other characters, thereby raising his status. Gerald would be standing downstage left, whereas Sheila would be on the opposite side of the stage, downstage right. I would place Sheila and Gerald either end of the large dining table, to show a physical barrier representing an emotional barrier. The exchange would continue across the table with the Inspector remaining in the centre but moving slightly downstage, not saying anything and allowing Gerald and Sheila to argue between themselves.

3 *Play*: An Inspector Calls
Scene: From where Birling looks triumphantly at everyone to the end of the play.
Scene title: Relief and cliffhanger
Theme 1: Responsibility
Ideas for establishing theme 1: Mr Birling repeats the key points from the case and Eric asks him not to, as he finds his part in the downfall uncomfortable. He covers his ears as Mr Birling speaks, shaking his head as if to deny it happened.
Theme 2: Generation and gender
Ideas for establishing theme 2: Mr Birling dismisses Sheila's concerns by saying she will have a good laugh about it. His superior attitude is shown by him treating Sheila as though she were still a small girl, laughing at her and not taking her seriously.

71. *An Inspector Calls*: plot

1 Act 1: The Birlings are celebrating the engagement of their daughter, Sheila, to Gerald Croft. A mysterious Inspector arrives to question them about the death of a young woman.
Act 2: Through hard questioning, Mrs Birling admits the girl came to her for money but she refused to help her.
Act 3: Gerald returns and indicates that he does not think Inspector Goole is a real police officer and that the family have been deceived.

2 **(a)** The dining room of the Birling house
(b) The engagement of their daughter, Sheila, to Gerald Croft

(c) While Gerald has the higher social status (coming from an aristocratic family), he is keen to show that he has total respect for Mr Birling. Even when Birling acknowledges the Croft family, Gerald shows that he is embarrassed, which again indicates that he wants to fit in with the family and is looking to avoid all areas of conflict.

3 (a) Daisy Renton

   (b) The first week of September

   (c) Sheila understands that the Inspector is laying a trap for each family member to fall into. She has seen how he worked with both her father and Gerald. She also understands that her mother is a very headstrong and forthright person who will naturally take great offence at the way in which the Inspector speaks to her (especially as she believes the Inspector to be of a lower status to herself). Sheila tries to save her mother from the inevitable embarrassment but fails to do so.

4 (a) Mr Birling

   (b) He telephones Colonel Roberts, the Chief Constable.

   (c) Set in 1912, a financially comfortable family are celebrating the engagement of their daughter. The evening takes a shocking turn when a mysterious Inspector arrives with some disturbing news that will change their relationships forever.

72. *Blue Stockings*: overview

1 (a) True; (b) True; (c) True; (d) True; (e) False (the play is set in 1896); (f) True; (g) False (the Senate votes against the motion for women to graduate from Cambridge University); (h) False (the play is structured into two acts, with a total of 25 scenes).

2 If I were directing this scene, I would place Mrs Welsh downstage centre, directly addressing the audience as though they were the members of the Senate. Not only would this draw the audience into the narrative, it would also show the huge task Mrs Welsh faces at this time. The stage direction indicates that the women are placed at the top of the stairs and so this would be done upstage right. The women would be waiting, looking nervous and trying to be positive as Maeve emerges onto the stage and walks past them. As Mrs Welsh then continues with her speech, I would have Maeve move downstage until she is adjacent to Mrs Welsh but positioned downstage right. She would get ready to face the final exit, just as Mrs Welsh is referring to Maeve, thus reinforcing yet another struggle young women faced at this time.

3 *Play*: Blue Stockings

   Scene: Act 1, Scene 12

   Scene title: Science of the Heart

   Theme 1: Balance

   Ideas for establishing theme 1: In an attempt to develop their learning further, Mr Banks pushes the men to explain the emotions behind their activities. As they begin to demonstrate understanding, Mr Banks becomes more animated and encouraging.

   Theme 2: Gender

   Ideas for establishing theme 2: As Edwards realises that the writer of the essay is female, there should be genuine shock in his voice, which is countered by Mr Banks who is pleased with his trap. This is further reinforced by Mr Banks referring to the men as 'boys' in his last line, which could be emphasised and preceded with a short pause.

73. *Blue Stockings*: plot

1 Act 1, Scene 4: The students gather to listen to a lecture from renowned scientist, Dr Maudsley.

   Act 1, Scene 8: Tess and Will meet in Tess's room. Will tries to warn Tess about her reputation. They argue and Will leaves.

   Act 2, Scene 6: Tess and Carolyn meet Holmes and Lloyd in a shop. Lloyd is unable to contain his disgust that women are being educated and launches into a vicious tirade against them.

   Act 2, Scene 11: During the vote, there is a violent protest against women being allowed to graduate. The vote is lost.

2 (a) Hysteria – why women are incapable of gaining an education.

   (b) She is furious about the way she was treated purely on the basis of her gender and also at the way in which Maudsley manipulated the situation to support his theories, making Tess look silly.

3 (a) She points out that that while science can explain how things work, the arts question why things work.

   (b) She believes the Suffragettes' strategy is too extreme and that a more patient, quiet approach, in which small advances are made, is more effective. She is concerned about the profile portrayed by the women gaining an education and does not wish to reinforce the image of women as projected by Dr Maudsley.

4 (a) A Suffragette rally.

   (b) While he is reflecting the views of many people of the time, he is also scared that women will show him up. Lloyd lists the amount of education he had, which has been denied to the women, and yet they are able to match his level of education regardless. Therefore, he feels very threatened.

5 (a) Vivas – a spoken examination. Collins and Radleigh ask the women a series of questions before informing them whether they have passed or failed.

   (b) Set in 1896, a group of young women studying at Girton College, Cambridge, fight to become the first females to have the right to graduate. Their struggles, both personal and professional, lead both genders to question what they really believe.

74. *The Crucible*: overview

1 (a) True; (b) True; (c) False (the first performance was in New York); (d) False (the play is set in 1692); (e) True; (f) True; (g) False (Abigail and the girls admit that the events had nothing to do with witchcraft); (h) False (the play is structured into four acts)

2 As a director, I would use a traditional 'end on' proscenium arch stage for this production. At the start of this section, I would place Cheever and Herrick at the door, which would be positioned stage left, to show they had just arrived and were the newcomers to the scene. Proctor and Elizabeth would be in the centre of the room, slightly upstage centre, with Elizabeth moving slightly behind Proctor when Cheever arrives. She would do this as she knows that his arrival is not good news for her and such a move would indicate that she is frightened and looking to her husband for protection. In addition, I would place Reverend Hale upstage right as this would help to indicate his status and provide him with a clear view downstage to the door. It would also indicate that, while Reverend Hale may not be fully welcome, the Proctors are respectful and show him courtesy by inviting him in to their home. Giles and Francis would balance the stage by being placed upstage left, where they can also look downstage towards Cheever.

3 *Play*: *The Crucible*
  Scene: Act 1: John and Abigail are alone for the first time.
  Scene title: John and Abigail
  Theme 1: Gender equality/inequality
  Ideas for establishing theme 1: Mercy Lewis shows fear and deference to Proctor as she leaves, sliding out of the door calling him 'Mr Proctor', whereas Abigail pointedly calls him 'John'. Abigail initially keeps her distance but then begins to move closer to John as she gains confidence.
  Theme 2: Betrayal
  Ideas for establishing theme 2: When Abigail grabs John's hand, he lets it linger for a little too long, even though he should immediately remove it. John initially flirts with Abigail, encouraging her by smiling at her.

75. *The Crucible*: plot

1 Act 1: Tituba confesses to witchcraft and names several women who she also claims work for the Devil.
   Act 2: Reverend Hale questions Proctor and Elizabeth about their Christian beliefs.
   Act 3: In court, Elizabeth denies that Proctor and Abigail had an affair, unknowingly supporting Abigail rather than her husband.
   Act 4: John Proctor confesses, then destroys his statement and is hanged.
2 **(a)** Betty Parris and Ruth Putnam
   (b) Tituba, being a slave, has the lowest status and will not be believed. The girls, who also have quite low status, know that Tituba is the only one who has a lower social standing than they do. Therefore, she is the only one they can blame and be believed.
3 **(a)** A poppet (doll)
   (b) She is afraid the girls will turn on her and accuse her of witchcraft. Mary also knows what happens to people when they are accused, having seen it and been a part of the process. She is fully aware that once accused there is no escape from the court.
4 **(a)** His affair with Abigail
   (b) Shocked, because her plan has backfired and the pressure she has put on Mary has led to Proctor being arrested and potentially hanged. Abigail is fully aware that once someone is accused there is little chance of them being pardoned. In addition to this, the only way to save Proctor is to admit that she and the other girls have been lying to the court – and that would mean she would be executed for murder.
5 **(a)** A dagger
   (b) Because he knows that by defying the authorities, he is standing up for truth and putting pressure on them to stop the trials. Proctor understands how the system works and that the only way he can now make his point is by sacrificing his life. He believes that by doing this he is helping to save the lives of others.

76. *DNA*: overview

1 **(a)** True; **(b)** True; **(c)** False (the first professional performance was at the Cottesloe Theatre of the National Theatre, London); **(d)** False (the location is not specified); **(e)** False (the exact time period is not specified); **(f)** True; **(g)** False (Phil takes Adam back to the hedge; soon after, Cathy and Phil return to the hedge to kill Adam); **(h)** False (the play is structured into four sections, with a total of 14 scenes)
2 If I were directing this scene, I would start by having John Tate try to intimidate Richard by squaring up to him and invading his personal space. As Richard physically tries

to defend himself, he should begin to look nervous. This would clearly indicate to the audience that John Tate does hold the upper hand. While John Tate then delivers his short monologue, he should circle Richard, keeping eye contact with the others to visually threaten them. Once he has fully circled Richard, John would end up slightly downstage, with his back to Richard, allowing Richard to step forward (as indicated in the stage directions) to try to reclaim some status, but his assertive body language would be undermined by his shaky voice.

3 *Play*: *DNA*
  Scene: Jan and Mark explain what the group did to Adam. Phil devises a plan to cover up the crime.
  Scene title: The explanation and the plan
  Theme 1: Bullying
  Ideas for establishing theme 1: As Jan and Mark both describe how the group assaulted Adam, in an attempt to justify what they were doing, the repeated use of the word 'laugh' and their recount of Adam laughing about the event, should be emphasised.
  Theme 2: Responsibility
  Ideas for establishing theme 2: While everyone is looking fearful and unsure what to do next, Phil should take centre stage and suddenly begin to speak with confidence and assurance. As he gives instructions, he should directly address each person, passing on the responsibility to them for their own part of the plan.

77. *DNA*: plot

1 Section 1: Phil outlines his plan to cover up the death of Adam, giving everyone in the group specific instructions.
   Section 2: A man is arrested for the abduction of Adam. His DNA matches the jumper, as Cathy has taken a jumper from a man fitting the description given to the police.
   Section 3: Weeks later, Adam is found alive. It is established that he has been living rough in a hedge.
   Section 4: Richard meets Brian alone in a field. He outlines the impact the events have had on everyone in the group.
2 **(a)** Because their combined weight will be similar to that of the fictional suspect, providing evidence of footprints in the mud.
   (b) Leah is an insecure character who is desperately trying to get Phil's attention. His silence is a mystery to her and she is constantly working to get a reaction, from putting herself down to trying to shock him.
3 **(a)** To take Brian to the grille and throw stones at him until he falls through and is killed, just like Adam.
   (b) Because the suspect described to the police was invented by Brian as part of the plan to cover up the death of Adam. The plan unravelled because Cathy thought she needed a jumper from a man who actually did match the description and so took one from the Sorting Office.
4 **(a)** Up the hill, living in a hedge.
   (b) Brian's fragile mental state means that he does not fully understand the consequences of his actions. By having Brian kill Adam, there is an opportunity for the others to distance themselves from the murder, as they are not the ones who actually kill Adam.
5 **(a)** He is now on stronger medication.
   (b) A group of teenagers, thinking they have killed someone, set in motion a plan to cover their crime. But when a man is arrested for the crime and then the victim turns up alive, their lives begin to unravel.

78. *Dr Korczak's Example*: overview

1 **(a)** True; **(b)** False (the first performance was in 2001); **(c)** False (the play was first performed as a tour in Scottish schools); **(d)** True; **(e)** False (the play is set in 1942, during the Nazi occupation of Poland); **(f)** True; **(g)** True; **(h)** False (the play is structured into 25 scenes).

2 If I were directing this scene, I would initially have Korczak and Cerniakov quite separate, despite them being old and close friends. As the meeting is taking place in Cerniakov's office, he will be sitting down, relatively relaxed. At the start, he gestures for Korczak to also sit, but the invitation is ignored, indicating the tension between the two of them. During the exchange regarding the rumours of what will happen to the children, Korczak would add a harsh, insistent tone when Cerniakov apparently brushes off his concerns. However, when Cerniakov gives Korczak his word that the children will not be harmed, Korczak visibly relaxes and then sits down, clearly showing that the initial tension has reduced and the trust between them has returned.

3 *Play*: Dr Korczak's Example
Scene: Scene 8 and Scene 9
Scene title: Catching flies and Meeting Stepan
Theme 1: Idealism
Ideas for establishing theme 1: Important decisions are referred to the Orphanage Council. Korczak should indicate some of the puppets or dolls, who are the members of the Council. When Stephanie needs the toilet, he again gestures to the Council and makes sure the rules, which have been set by the children, are followed.
Theme 2: Religious tolerance
Ideas for establishing theme 2: It should be made obvious that Stepan, a Christian, is not wearing the yellow armband and therefore this distinguishes him as non-Jewish. Korczak may greet his friend with energy and hold Stepan's arm where the armband would be (to draw attention to its absence).

79. *Dr Korczak's Example*: plot

1 Scene 4: Adzio is introduced to the orphanage and meets Dr Korczak.
Scene 9: Stepan, a Christian, offers Dr Korczak an escape from the ghetto. It would mean abandoning the children so Dr Korczak refuses.
Scene 18: Adzio and Stephanie, angry with the priest for not letting the children play in the church garden, throw stones at the church windows, breaking them.
Scene 21: Cerniakov, discovering that the children will be transported to the camps, is devastated and commits suicide.

2 **(a)** The sewers
(b) He has had to survive on the streets against the Nazi regime. He has seen that, as fear increases, people are only looking after themselves rather than helping each other.

3 **(a)** He must give Bruno his bread rations for three days.
(b) The soldier represents the violence and fear that surrounds the children and stops them from developing into rounded, mature, civilised people who can find non-aggressive ways to resolve their differences.

4 **(a)** A fat toad
(b) He has a great fear of the Nazis and does not want to risk any repercussions of being associated with the Jewish community.

5 **(a)** They will be executed on the spot.
(b) He is a man of principle. By standing together with the children, he sets an example of refusing to accept a way of life under an oppressive regime.

80. *Government Inspector*: overview

1 **(a)** True; **(b)** True; **(c)** False (the first performance took place in St Petersburg, Russia); **(d)** False (the play is set in 19th-century Russia); **(e)** True; **(f)** True; **(g)** True; **(h)** False (the play is structured into five acts).

2 If I were directing this scene, I would place Khlestakov and Osip downstage left, making them the initial focus for the audience. The set I would use to represent the Mayor's house would be grand with large windows. However, those windows would be opaque and allow for shadow theatre to be used. As the shopkeepers approach, the audience will be able to see the silhouette of the crowd as they gather. To give the impression of them getting closer, and therefore raising the tension level, I would then have them move towards the light source – making their shadows bigger. At the same time I would increase the noise level, allowing it to build to a climax. To add to this, I would have Osip reacting with increasing nervousness and fear, which again would convey the rising tension to the audience.

3 *Play*: Government Inspector
Scene: Act 4, Scene 2
Scene title: Bribery
Theme 1: Mistaken identity
Ideas for establishing theme 1: As Zemlyanika enters the room, he should have an air of confidence that he knows he is speaking with someone of importance, but that he has information which raises his own status. As he informs on his colleagues, he moves towards Khlestakov, believing he has gained favour with this powerful man.
Theme 2: Corruption
Ideas for establishing theme 2: Khlestakov no longer feels the need to be concerned about the evident bribery. As Zemlyanika speaks, he is only just pretending to be interested. Once he has all of the information he feels Zemlyanika wants to give him, he openly asks for money, which should be physically reinforced by holding out his hand and clicking his fingers, as if he expects an immediate response.

81. *Government Inspector*: plot

1 Act 1: The Mayor, panicking because a Government Inspector has arrived, orders the officials of the town to clean everything up.
Act 2: The Mayor and Khlestakov meet. The Mayor believes that Khlestakov is a Government Inspector.
Act 3: Khlestakov is welcomed into the Mayor's house and meets Anna and Maria.
Act 4: The officials of the town are individually introduced to Khlestakov and nervously bribe him.
Act 5: Khlestakov and Osip escape before the truth is discovered. The people realise they have been deceived.

2 The Mayor knows how much corruption is going on in the town, and realises that he could be in serious trouble if it is discovered that he encourages such criminality. Therefore, he is desperate to cover up as much as possible.

3 Khlestakov has no money and has been conning the hotel into providing him with food and drink without paying for them. This is a pattern he has been following from town to town. He believes that he is about to be caught and punished for his debts, and he makes (inaccurate) assumptions about why the Mayor wants to speak with him.

4   Maria is a young and impressionable girl who has innocent ideas about romance and love. She is looking for her perfect partner and is looking to impress Khlestakov. Anna believes that, even though she is older and married, men still find her attractive and she is keen to show off to Khlestakov, whom she considers to be refined and of high social standing. The women constantly bicker, therefore, as they are both trying to get the upper hand in this situation.

5   Lyapkin-Tyapkin is nervous because he believes that Khlestakov, whom he thinks is the Government Inspector, will uncover his corrupt approach to justice and punish him. In addition to this, he plans to bribe Khlestakov, but Lyapkin-Tyapkin knows this is a very risky strategy that could seriously backfire if Khlestakov does not take kindly to this corruption.

6   Corrupt officials of a small Russian town discover that a Government Inspector will visit them. Assuming the stranger staying in town is the Inspector, they lavish him with bribes. But is the 'Inspector' the person they think he is?

82. *Twelfth Night*: overview

1   **(a)** False (William Shakespeare wrote *Twelfth Night*); **(b)** False (it was first performed in the early 17th century); **(c)** True; **(d)** True; **(e)** False (the title is a reference to the Festival of Twelfth Night – held during midwinter – where traditional roles, including those of status and gender, were often inverted); **(f)** True; **(g)** False (Malvolio would like more power, but he is a steward in Olivia's household); **(h)** True

2   As a director, I would place Malvolio downstage centre, to make him the focus of the audience's attention. The letter would be slightly off centre, towards stage right, so as to give Malvolio time to outline his desires to be 'Count Malvolio' and married to Olivia before seeing the letter. The box hedge would be placed upstage right and angled to enable the audience to see the characters behind the hedge. Malvolio should spend his time with his back to the hedge, emphasising to the audience that he is unaware of the other characters there. This physical barrier will also enable them to speak to each other and indicate that Malvolio cannot hear them.

3   *Play*: Twelfth Night
    Scene: Act 4, Scene 1
    Scene title: Sir Andrew and Sebastian
    Theme 1: Ambition
    Ideas for establishing theme 1: Sir Andrew's ambition to impress Olivia by beating Cesario is rekindled when he meets Sebastian (who he mistakes for Cesario). By making eye contact and gesturing by pointing towards Sebastian, the audience will see that he recognises Sebastian. He may enhance this by rubbing his hands together as he acknowledges this is his opportunity.
    Theme 2: Love
    Ideas for establishing theme 2: When Oliva rushes in to find Sir Toby pointing his drawn sword at Sebastian, she must rush between them, thinking Sebastian is Cesario. She would stand, wide arms outstretched and facing Sir Toby, as though protecting Sebastian and using her status to defeat Sir Toby. In this way, Olivia demonstrates to the audience that she is willing to put herself in danger to protect the one she loves.

83. *Twelfth Night*: plot

1   Act 1: Viola is saved from a shipwreck and disguises herself as a man to gain employment with Orsino.
    Act 2: Malvolio finds a letter, supposedly from Olivia,

but actually it is a trick played on him by Sir Toby, Sir Andrew, Maria, Fabian and Feste.
    Act 3: Sir Andrew challenges Cesario (Viola) to a duel in an attempt to impress Olivia.
    Act 4: Olivia mistakes Sebastian for Cesario, helping and caring for him – which is very confusing for Sebastian, as he has never met her before!
    Act 5: Viola and Sebastian are reunited and true identities are revealed. Olivia and Sebastian, Orsino and Viola, Sir Toby and Maria all get married.

2   Sir Toby refers to the fact that Sir Andrew is a wealthy man. By making him stay, Sir Toby will benefit from Sir Andrew's money, enabling him to carry on with his drunken lifestyle.

3   Malvolio is seen as a killjoy and disliked by all of the characters. When Malvolio threatens to undermine Maria in front of Olivia, Maria is angered and devises a plan to get revenge on Malvolio by making him believe Olivia is in love with him. However, Maria's plot will actually humiliate Malvolio instead.

4   While Malvolio thinks he is carrying out Olivia's instructions, she actually has no idea why he is behaving so strangely. Olivia is concerned that Malviolio is not behaving seriously and her concern increases when he answers her questions inappropriately.

5   Olivia believes Sebastian is Cesario, with whom she is in love. She naturally takes his side and uses her high status to protect him. However, Sebastian doesn't know about Cesario, or Olivia's confusion, so is confused himself.

6   In this tale of shipwrecks, dukes, counts and drunken uncles, a young woman attempts to find her lost brother. Yet, while disguised as a man to protect her identity, she ends up finding a lot more than she bargained for!

TIMED TEST

Where an exemplar answer is given, this is not necessarily the only correct response. In most cases, there is a range of responses that can gain full marks. Example answers are based on one of the eight possible performance texts for Edexcel GCSE Drama.

Note: The page numbers below refer to the Section A **answer** pages. To remind yourself of the Section A questions in the timed test, turn to the relevant pages for your performance text:
1984 – pages 85–86
An Inspector Calls – pages 87–88
Blue Stockings – pages 89–90
The Crucible – pages 91–92
DNA – pages 93–94
Dr Korczak's Example – pages 95–96
Government Inspector – pages 97–98
Twelfth Night – pages 99–100

102. Section A, Question (a)(i)

The question asks you to explain two ways you would use either physical skills or vocal skills to play the selected character. You need to:
- justify your ideas by linking them to the text extract
- include specific examples and quotations where appropriate.

Answers might consider the following:
(i) Physical skills
Movement:
- Using movement and style of walking to show the age/status/context of the character, such as swaying, crawling, tripping, striding, skipping, running or shuffling.

- Pulling/pushing other characters to indicate the context or status of the character.
- Carrying or dragging an item to indicate the weight of the item or physical strength of the character.
- Leaning on other characters to indicate the status of the character or the physicality of the character being played.

Gesture:
- Using hand gestures to reinforce a key point, such as bending over with hands on knees to indicate being out of breath, pointing at a location or character.
- Holding out both hands in front to indicate stop or surrender.
- Waving to indicate an arrival or departure of a character.

For example, an answer about physical skills for *Twelfth Night* (the duke, Act 2, Scene 4) might be:

I would enter slowly dragging my feet, feeling huge heartache for the unreturned love of Olivia.

Then when Feste enters, I would quickly perk up, raising my head and turning towards him and beckoning, showing that his song is the only thing that can relieve my pain.

(ii) Vocal skills

Tone of delivery:
- Indicating stage direction, such as 'hesitantly' by using pause, 'with embarrassment' by mumbling, 'excitedly' by speaking quickly with a high-pitched voice or 'hurriedly' by speaking quickly but with a lower, serious tone.
- Highlighting the emotions experienced by the character, such as joy, excitement, happiness or fear.
- Portraying an inner conflict, for example, by using one type of tone when speaking to a character on stage but a different tone when directly addressing the audience or delivering a monologue.
- Demonstrating relationships between the characters, for example, if a character likes another the tone of voice would be friendly; if there is conflict between two people the tone maybe angry or harsh.

Pace of delivery:
- Using fast or slow delivery.
- Using pauses to indicate thinking time or a difficult relationship.
- Changing pace to show a change within the character.
- Adopting a smooth or clipped, staccato delivery to indicate character traits.

For example, an answer about vocal skills for *DNA* (Lou in Section 2) might be:

At the start of the scene, I would use a very tight, quavering tone of voice, showing that I know all the information being shared with Leah, but also that I am trying to control my fear.

Throughout the middle section, I would raise the volume of my voice and quicken the pace, indicating my frustration that she doesn't understand the situation as quickly as I want her to.

103. Section A, Question (a)(ii)

The question asks you to give three suggestions of how you would use performance skills to play the selected character. You need to:

- justify your ideas by linking them to the text extract
- include specific examples and quotations where appropriate.

Answers might consider the following:

Physicality:
- Demonstrating an understanding of the stage directions included in the extract, such as moving to a specific part of the stage.
- Considering the exact part of the stage from where a character enters and/or exits (if relevant).
- Using gesture to highlight a key point or draw attention to a specific part of the stage or character.
- Varying movement across the stage, including the pace, style of movement and what the movement might represent (for example, if someone is injured or overtly happy).
- Using posture, which may indicate age, status or context.
- Using facial expression to portray character emotion, relationships, subtext or an inner conflict, for example.

Vocal skills:
- Varying tone and intonation of voice to indicate emotion and context.
- Using pace, pause and silence to indicate the context in which the character finds themselves.
- Using vocal effects, such as sobbing, gasping, stammering, pace of breathing (for instance, taking shallow breaths to show fear).
- Experimenting with accent to indicate location, background or status.

Use of space:
- Use of proxemics to explore relationships and status, for example, if two characters like each other they might stand close together; if they are arguing they may stand far apart.
- Use of levels to indicate status, location and context; for example, a high status character may be raised higher than others, whereas someone with low status may be placed lower.

For example, an answer for *Government Inspector* (Khlestakov, Act 3, Scene 4) might be:

To show Khlestakov's growing exaggeration, I would deliver the monologue as though it were a great, epic story, using rising and falling intonation to highlight the important moments, and pausing just before key words.

As Khlestakov grows in confidence, I would move closer to Anna and establish clear and strong eye contact. This would show that I am flirting with her, which would raise my status in the room as I would be doing so in front of her husband.

I would use gesture throughout the monologue. For example, when Khlestakov says he is refusing promotion, I would raise my palms upwards and outwards as if in protest, following this with a sweeping gesture when talking about walking past the desks of co-workers. I would allow the gesture to flow into putting my arm around Anna, again indicating my growing confidence.

104. Section A, Question (b)(i)

The question asks you to focus on the use of one production element from the perspective of a director. You need to discuss how the production element you have chosen would bring the selected extract to life for an audience. The audience must be at the heart of your response. You need to:

- justify your ideas by linking them to the text extract
- include specific examples and quotations where appropriate.

Your answer might consider the following:

Costume:
- Showing time period and/or status.
- Representing or symbolising key aspects of the character and/or narrative.
- Using colours to highlight key information.
- Using different materials.

Lighting:
- Enhancing mood or atmosphere.
- Indicating location.
- Indicating time of day or time of year (such as a red glow to indicate late evening).

Props/stage furniture:
- Indicating time period/era, such as a mobile phone or a quill.
- Reflecting location, such as a bed to represent a hotel room or a large wooden cross to represent a church.
- Reflecting character traits or professions, such as a character's notebook or sword.

Set:
- Styling the set, such as symbolic, minimalistic or naturalistic.
- Using levels to indicate status.
- Using symbolism to indicate locations and time period.
- Using colour to indicate and/or represent key information to an audience.

Sound:
- Using sound effects, either recorded or live.
- Using music to set mood or atmosphere (such as building tension at key moments).
- Playing historically accurate music, reflecting the era in which the performance is set.
- Making specific sound effects to indicate key moments and events, such as a door creaking open, thunder rolling or footsteps approaching.

Staging:
- Using entrances and exits to indicate different off-stage locations.
- Creating and building up performer–audience relationships.
- Considering sightlines and blocking.
- Using staging, such as proscenium arch, theatre-in-the-round or traverse theatr.

For example, an answer about costume for *An Inspector Calls* might start like this:

As a director, I would want the costume to indicate both the 20th century time period to the audience, as well as the status and age of the characters. For example, both Mrs Birling and Sheila would wear long evening gowns, reflecting the formality of the evening as well as the wealth of the family. In line with this, I would want Mr Birling and Eric to be dressed in dinner jackets with bow ties. However, to show the difference between the generations, I would direct Mr Birling to keep his bow tie formally tied, but Eric to wear his loose…

106. Section A, Question (b)(ii)

The question asks you to make decisions about characterisation from the perspective of a director. You need to discuss how a director would work with a performer to deliver specific character traits within the extract. The audience must be at the heart of your response. Your answer should:
- demonstrate your knowledge of voice and physicality, as well as stage directions and stage space
- show a clear understanding of how these elements support your ideas and the requirements for the character in the extract given.

Your answer might consider the following:

Voice:
- Delivering specific lines in order to convey the required character trait (such as high/low status, fear, excitement, deference or exclusion).

- Using pause/silence, as well as tone, volume, pace, pitch and intonation to create dramatic meaning for the audience.

Physicality:
- Using body language and gesture during specific moments of the extract to convey specific character traits.
- Using personal props to enhance physicality, such as a walking stick to indicate frailty or a cane to highlight status.

Stage directions and stage space:
- Selecting specific areas of the stage to indicate status/authority.
- Using proxemics with other characters to highlight relationships.
- Using levels and audience awareness to convey subtext or conflicting views, such as revealing the character's true feelings regarding a secret to the audience while maintaining a different point of view to the other characters on stage.

For example, an answer for *1984* that focused on The Host at the end of the play might start like this:

As a director, I would instruct the performer playing The Host to show the audience the high status that comes with having more knowledge than the other characters. Therefore, I would direct The Host to take the book and close it as he confirms that is how the story ends. During the next few lines, I would direct him to move away from the other performers, who would be crowded together downstage centre, and to upstage right, emphasising his higher status. I would also want to make The Host seem subtly different to the other characters, so when The Host says that Winston was 'imagined', I would direct him to look directly at Winston, acknowledging him for the first and only time…

108. Section A, Question (c)

The question asks you, as a designer, to discuss how you would use one design element to enhance the production of the given extract for an audience. You need to indicate how you would use your chosen element, as well as demonstrate your understanding of how that element can enhance the production. You need to:
- justify your ideas by linking them to the text extract
- include specific examples and quotations where appropriate.

If relevant, you may also wish to make a linked comment relating to a different design element, to show how this would further enhance the element you have chosen to write about. For example, if your answer focused on set design, you could make a very brief reference to colours within the lighting that would have an impact on the colours/effects used in the set.

Your answer might consider the following:

Costume:
- Showing time period and/or status.
- Representing or symbolising key aspects of the character and/or narrative.
- Using colours to highlight key information.
- Using different materials.

Lighting:
- Enhancing mood or atmosphere.
- Indicating location.
- Indicating time of day or time of year (such as a red glow to indicate late evening).

Props/stage furniture:
- Using props to indicate time period/era, such as a mobile phone or a quill.

- Reflecting location, for example, a large table to represent a dining room or crockery to represent a canteen.
- Reflecting character traits or professions, such as a character's notebook or sword.

Set:
- Styling the set, such as symbolic, minimalistic or naturalistic.
- Using levels to indicate status.
- Using symbolism to indicate locations and time period.
- Using colour to indicate and/or represent key information to the audience.

Sound:
- Using sound effects, either recorded or live.
- Playing music to set mood or atmosphere (such as building tension at key moments).
- Using historically accurate music to reflect the era in which the performance is set.
- Using specific sound effects to indicate key moments and events, such as a door creaking open, thunder rolling or footsteps approaching.

Staging:
- Using entrances and exits to indicate different off-stage locations.
- Creating and building up performer–audience relationships.
- Considering sightlines and blocking.
- Using staging, such as proscenium arch, theatre-in-the-round or traverse theatre.

For example, an answer about lighting for *Dr Korczak's Example* might start like this:

As a lighting designer for this extract, I would use lighting to help with the challenges of using puppets, which cannot move by themselves, to represent different characters. For example, at the start of Scene 10, I would use a dim, yellowing spotlight above Dr Korczak as he sits at his desk. This would represent the early sunlight of the morning as well as the isolation he feels at being trapped in the ghetto. The pool of light, shone from above the front of the stage, will give light to the performer and be large enough for Stephanie to move into as well. During the exchange with Adzio, I would fade up a very deep blue wash at the rear of the performance area. The performer playing Stephanie can then enter this area and begin to arrange the puppets into their positions for the following court scene, while the discussion between Adzio and Dr Korczak takes place...

Note: The page numbers below refer to the Section B **answer** pages. To remind yourself of the Section B questions in the timed test, turn to page 101.

110. Section B, Question 9(a)

The question asks you to analyse either a performance element or a design element of a live performance you have seen. You must include specific examples from across the live performance to help justify your answer.

(i) Design element

For the specific question in this timed test (about how levels were used in the staging of the performance), answers might consider how:
- specific characters were raised higher to indicate high status
- characters were placed lower to indicate low status
- characters were placed higher up to demonstrate vulnerability or that they were being controlled and being told where to go

- specific technical language was used, relating to set and staging.

For questions about other design elements, answers might consider, for example:
- use of colours, materials or shapes to convey meaning and information
- an understanding of the style and genre of the design elements in the context of the performance
- how the selected design element has an impact on a range of performance aspects, such as creation of mood, tension, atmosphere, to show relationships, to engage the audience, to indicate character/status, to indicate time period/setting.

For example, an answer for this design question, using the National Theatre's 2011 production of *Frankenstein* (with Jonny Lee Miller as The Creature) might be:

The staging for this production was mainly on one level, though status was indicated to the audience using upstage and downstage areas. For example, when The Creature first arrived in Geneva, he met a young boy. The Creature, nervous of how people react to him, approached the boy from the upstage area and initially refused to let the boy turn around. This is indicated clearly how The Creature was attempting to keep his status, as well as reinforcing his fear of interacting with humans.

Another key moment was when Frankenstein told Elizabeth he was going to England. At this point the set for the study emerged from the floor and was raised on an angle with the stage right area being higher than stage left. While Frankenstein told Elizabeth he was leaving and that she was less 'educated' than him, he was positioned higher up. Elizabeth, clearly accepting that Frankenstein as her intellectual superior, stayed lower down on the stage left part of the set. However, as she began to question Frankenstein and answer each of his comments, she started to move stage right while he moved stage left. This resulted in them quickly changing positions, indicating to Frankenstein – and the audience – that she was not as 'inferior' as he might like to think. This is also a moment where the characters become slightly closer, both physically and emotionally, which was reflected in their physical positions on stage.

(ii) Performance element

For the specific question in this timed test (which refers to how body language was used to convey relationships between characters at a key moment in the performance), answers might consider how:
- specific gestures were used by the performers
- performers used proxemics
- performers made physical contact with each other
- performers leaned forwards or backwards to represent how they felt about another character.

For questions about other performance elements, answers might consider:
- an analysis of physical skills
- an analysis of vocal skills
- how the performer used space, staging and levels
- an understanding of proxemics
- how the selected performance techniques contributed to conveying a range of aspects, such as creation of mood, tension and atmosphere, to show relationships, to indicate character/status, to engage the audience.

For example, an answer for this performance question, using the National Theatre's 2011 production of *Frankenstein* (with Jonny Lee Miller as The Creature), might be:

A key moment in the performance was where The Creature finally revealed himself to Frankenstein. Throughout this section, the relationship between the two characters changed as Frankenstein began to understand more about The Creature, and the performers used strong body language to convey these changes to the audience.

For example, during the physical struggle, The Creature held down Frankenstein, who was initially frightened of him. To show this, the performer, Benedict Cumberbatch, constantly wriggled in an attempt to get free and move away from The Creature's face. However, when The Creature, played by Jonny Lee Miller, started to quote from *Paradise Lost*, Frankenstein began to be intrigued by how advanced The Creature was. Therefore, Cumberbatch stopped struggling, relaxing his body language. The following exchange between the two was a battle to try to gain the higher moral ground. The body language between them was aggressive, each circling the other and pointedly gesturing at each other. This continued until The Creature's anger burst out and he violently attacked Frankenstein by grabbing his throat and dragging him to the ground. The Creature instantly regreted his actions, which was demonstrated by Miller releasing Cumberbatch, withdrawing, and bowing his head in shame.

112. Section B, Question 9(b)

The question asks you to evaluate either a performance element or a design element of a live performance you have seen. You must include specific examples from across the performance to help justify your answer.

(i) Performance element

For the specific question in this timed test (about how performance skills were used to create mood), answers might consider:

- a specific key moment of the performance
- how the performers used the required skills (performance skills in this case)
- clear examples to link and support the answer given
- how the performance skills had an impact on the mood of the specific key moment.

For example, an answer for this performance question, using the National Theatre's 2011 production of *Frankenstein* (with Jonny Lee Miller as The Creature), might start like this:

A key moment in the performance was when the old man introduced The Creature, played by Jonny Lee Miller, to his family. During this sequence, Miller selected and controlled his body language and voice to show the vulnerability of The Creature to the audience. While The Creature was being beaten by the old man's son, Miller used clumsy, uncontrolled movements which reminded the audience of a young child that has just learned to walk. The performer's exaggerated, uncontrolled, gestures to defend his body while trying to gallop away from the attack made us feel sympathy for The Creature. Miller's performance skills at this point were highly effective, especially when contrasted with the son's violent and yet controlled attack…

(ii) Design element

For the specific question in this timed test (about how volume in the performance was used to create atmosphere), answers might:

- compare different moments from the performance
- consider how sound was used in the performance
- give clear examples to link and support the answer given
- provide a positive or negative evaluation of how sound was used in the production
- focus on how sound was used to create atmosphere.

For example, an answer for this design question, using the National Theatre's 2011 production of *Frankenstein* (with Jonny Lee Miller as The Creature), might start like this:

One of the most powerful examples of how volume had an impact on the atmosphere of the performance was near the beginning of the play, as The Creature was emerging and learning to walk. Rhythmical music, with an African tribal feel to it, created a very positive and exciting, atmosphere. This reflected the idea that we were witnessing the birth of a new 'species'. As The Creature grew in strength, so did the music, using crescendo and almost overwhelming the audience. The atmosphere became quite uncomfortable at this point, because, although the music was still positive, it felt as though there was no escape. Again, this reflected the birth, and how The Creature was also overwhelmed by the sensations he was experiencing for the first time…

Published by Pearson Education Limited, 80 Strand, London, WC2R 0RL.

www.pearsonschoolsandfecolleges.co.uk

Copies of official specifications for all Pearson qualifications may be found on the website: qualifications.pearson.com

Text and illustrations © Pearson Education Ltd 2017
Typeset and illustrated by Kamae Design
Produced by Out of House Publishing
Cover illustration by Miriam Sturdee

The right of William Reed to be identified as author of this work has been asserted by him in accordance with the Copyright, Designs and Patents Act 1988.

First published 2017

20 19 18 17
10 9 8 7 6 5 4 3 2 1

British Library Cataloguing in Publication Data
A catalogue record for this book is available from the British Library

ISBN 978 1 292 13197 9

Acknowledgements
The author and publisher would like to thank the following individuals and organisations for permission to reproduce photographs:

(Key: b-bottom; c-centre; l-left; r-right; t-top)

123RF: Romvo 67cb; **Photolibrary.com:** Don Farrall 67bc; **Photostage:** Donald Cooper 1c, 36l, 46bc, 50r, 50l, 56t, 56b; **Royal Shakespeare Company:** Photo by Helen Maybanks © RSC 1b; **Shutterstock:** GlebStock 1t, Sherwood 46t, Elisanth 46tc, Arman Zhenikeyev 52l, Gabrielle Ewart 52r, Ksander 67t, Ignite Lab 67tc, HSNphotography 67ct, Roman Sakhno 67b; **Topfoto:** Johan Persson/ArenaPal 36r, Marcelo Bendehan/ArenaPal 46b

All other images © Pearson Education Ltd

Notes from the publisher
1. While the publishers have made every attempt to ensure that advice on the qualification and its assessment is accurate, the official specification and associated assessment guidance materials are the only authoritative source of information and should always be referred to for definitive guidance.

   Pearson examiners have not contributed to any sections in this resource relevant to examination papers for which they have responsibility.

2. Pearson has robust editorial processes, including answer and fact checks, to ensure the accuracy of the content in this publication, and every effort is made to ensure this publication is free of errors. We are, however, only human, and occasionally errors do occur. Pearson is not liable for any misunderstandings that arise as a result of errors in this publication, but it is our priority to ensure that the content is accurate. If you spot an error, please do contact us at resourcescorrections@pearson.com so we can make sure it is corrected.